Indira Gandhi
Speeches and Writings

Indira Gandhi
Speeches and Writings

HARPER & ROW, PUBLISHERS

New York, Evanston, San Francisco, London

This work was originally published under the title
India: The Speeches and Reminiscences of Indira Gandhi.

FIRST U.S. EDITION

Library of Congress Cataloging in Publication Data

Gandhi, Indira Nehru, 1917-   Indira Gandhi, speeches & writings.

   Originally published under title: India, the speeches and reminiscences of Indira Gandhi.
   Includes index.
   1.   India—Politics and government—1947-   —Collected works.   2.   India—Foreign relations—Collected works.   3.   Gandhi, Indira Nehru, 1917-   I.   Title.
DS480.84.G268   1975   954.04′092′4   75-4268
ISBN 0-06-011407-X

75 76 77 78 79 10 9 8 7 6 5 4 3 2 1

The author and publishers would like to acknowledge the assistance of H. Y. Sharada Prasad and K. Natwar-Singh.

तत्त्वमेव जयते

PRIME MINISTER

Foreword

Through the vicissitudes of Indian history, the fact stands out that unity does not necessarily connote uniformity and life cannot be imprisoned in a single theory. India has drawn sustenance from its diversity and strength from its seeming weakness. The haste of contemporary journalism and the tendency of modern scholarship to specialise rather than synthesise, makes India a difficult country to understand.

The upsurge of nationalism under Mahatma Gandhi's guidance enabled many of us to attune ourselves intuitively to this central fact of the Indian spirit. Jawaharlal Nehru's articulation made it an intellectually tangible reality. As Prime Minister for almost nine years, I have been continuously aware that my function, while drawing up and working out a programme of action to lighten the burden of poverty and inherited injustice, is to preserve the life-giving and creative diversity of India. This same concern enlivens our foreign policy.

Being my father's daughter it was inevitable that I should be fascinated by the uniqueness of India and her many-faceted personality and deeply committed (to the extent of merging my identity) to the welfare of her people. Even that was not an end but a necessary step towards making the country realise its potential. By this I mean neither military power, wealth nor status in the hierarchy of nations. I mean greatness of spirit where the rich heritage of centuries is nourished by growing scientific knowledge and new experience.

I hope this selection of speeches will give readers a glimpse of this deeper preoccupation and help towards an understanding of our immediate problems. The editors have also included a few autobiographical sketches— reminders of a time when cares were fewer!

Indira Gandhi

New Delhi, November 19, 1974

Contents

Chapter One: Reminiscences   page
   1. Childhood   13
   2. My Sixteenth Year   15
   3. A Page from the Book of Memory   16

Chapter Two: Gandhi and Nehru
   1. My Reminiscences of "Bapu"   23
   2. Mahatma Gandhi   25
   3. Jawaharlal Nehru: the foreword to the *Selected Works*   29
   4. Jawaharlal Nehru—a tribute   31

Chapter Three: Family Life
   1. On Being a Hostess   37
   2. On Being a Mother   41
   3. India Today   44

Chapter Four: Speeches, 1966-1970
   1. Broadcast to the Nation   51
   2. Address at Madras University, 1967   55
   3. Convocation Address at Santiniketan   62
   4. Convocation Address at Roorkee University   65
   5. On A Doctor's Work   72
   6. Family Planning   77
   7. Can India Survive?   80
   8. Convocation Address at the Kashi Vidyapith   88

Chapter Five: The Congress Party   page
   1. Introduction   97
   2. The Role of the Congress Party   98
   3. Open Letter to Members of the Congress Party   111

Chapter Six: Foreign Policy and the United Nations
   1. UN Conference on Trade and Development, 1968   119
   2. UN General Assembly, 1968   124
   3. Foreign Policy Determinants, 1970   131
   4. Non-Aligned Countries Conference, Lusaka, 1970   141
   5. UN General Assembly, 1970   147
   6. Foreign Affairs, 1971   154
   7. National Press Club, Washington, 1971   162

Chapter Seven: Indo-Pakistan War: Birth of Bangla Desh, 1971
   1. Introduction   169
   2. Prime Minister's Broadcast to the Nation   170
   3. Open Letter to Mr. Richard Nixon   171
   4. Prime Minister's Statement   174
   5. Cease-Fire on Western Front   175

Chapter Eight: Speeches, 1971-1972
   1. Democracy in India   181
   2. Political Science   185
   3. Human Environment   191

Chapter Nine: Twenty-Five Years of Independence, 1947-1972
   1. Article for *Foreign Affairs*   203
   2. Speech at Midnight Session of Parliament,
      August 14-15, 1972   215

Index   217

CHAPTER ONE

Reminiscences

1. CHILDHOOD*

"YOU WERE THE PROUDEST LOOKING BABY I HAVE SEEN," SAID Mrs. Naidu† of our first meeting. It was when I was six months old and in my grandmother's arms, waiting at the top of the steps to receive our guest.

My own first memory is of the day when, in response to Gandhiji's appeal, all over the country, foreign clothes were burnt. I can still feel the excitement of the day and see the large terrace covered with piles of clothes —what rich materials, what lovely colours! What fun for a toddler to jump on, play hide and seek in the heaps of velvets and satins, silks and chiffons! That was the day too when I discovered my power over my parents. Everybody was going to the bonfire but I was considered too small and was being put to bed. I appealed to my grandfather, who, then as always later, took my side. However, I fell asleep almost as soon as we arrived, seeing only the burning wood being thrown on the mountain of clothes and the fire putting forth its first flickering testing tongue of flame.

A little later took place my first encounter with conscience and duty. Being an only child, I liked playing by myself but I liked to have my mother within my range of vision and hearing. One evening she had a visitor, a relative returning from Paris who had brought an exquisite embroidered dress for me. Mummy smilingly returned it saying that we now wore only handspun and handwoven material. The visitor could not

*This article was written for a school magazine, in November 1957.

†Mrs. Sarojini Naidu (1879–1949): first Indian woman to take a degree at Cambridge, a friend and supporter of Mahatma Gandhi from 1914 till his assassination in 1948. She was President of the Indian National Congress (1925) and was well-known as a poet, orator and wit. She once teased Gandhi by telling him how much it cost to keep him poor. She was also a close friend of the Nehru family. After Independence she became Governor of India's most populous state, Uttar Pradesh.

understand this, and glancing at my mother's clothes—the only *khadi* available then was thick and rough as sacking—she could not help noticing that wherever her skin had rubbed against the sari it had become sore and red. She burst out, "I think you have all gone mad but you are adult, and if you want to be ill, I suppose that is your business, but you certainly have no right to make the child suffer and it is for her that I have brought this gift." "Come here, Indu," called my mother, "Aunty has brought you a foreign frock. It is very pretty and you can wear it if you like but first think of the big fire where we burnt our foreign things. Would you like to wear this dainty thing when the rest of us are wearing *khadi*?" The temptation was very strong—my eyes shone with desire—I stretched out a small hand to touch the dress but even before my hand reached it I found myself saying "Take it away—I shan't ever wear it." "But why not, don't you like nice things?" the visitor teased. "I do ... I do ... but ..." and I repeated all the arguments I had overheard from the elders' talk, when she said, "All right, Miss Saint, how is it that you have a foreign doll?" It was an idle remark, thoughtlessly made. Adults so often look upon children as playthings—not understanding what is hidden by the lack of power of expression. I was passionately fond of the doll, I could not think of it, or indeed of anything, as lifeless. Everything was given a name and immediately developed its own personality—the doll was my friend, my child.

For days on end—or was it weeks? Does it matter? It was eternity to the child, overwhelmed by the burden of decision. The struggle between love of the doll and pride in the ownership of such a lovely thing—and, as I thought, duty towards my country. Never fond of food, at this time it became even more irksome and sleep came only out of exhaustion. My mother thought I was sickening for something and so I was. At last the decision was made and, quivering with tension, I took the doll up on the roof-terrace and set fire to her. Then the tears came as if they could never stop and for some days I was ill with a temperature! To this day I hate striking a match!

Our house was beginning its new career of being a centre for political activities. There were constant meetings, big and small. My favourite game was to collect as many servants as I could, stand on a table and deliver a speech—repeating disjointed phrases that I had picked up from grown-up talk.

2. MY SIXTEENTH YEAR*

Returning home from an exhausting tour is a mixed blessing, for one dreads the inevitable accumulation of files. *Roshni's* request was a welcome change.

My sixteenth year was greeted by the not unusual occurrence of my father's arrest. He sent a telegram—"going to other home". My mother was ill. I was troubled and anxious but was occupied with my studies and dance practice, for I took my matriculation exam just then and made a brief appearance for the only time on the stage of a regular theatre.

When I left for good, practically the entire school including some parents accompanied me on the suburban train to say goodbye at Victoria Terminus. Old songs were sung amidst mingled tears and laughter.

I had wanted to be a boy but at sixteen the delight of being a woman began to unfold itself and almost overnight, the long-legged tomboy in frocks changed into a sari-clad young lady. I came to Calcutta to be with my mother and to share with her the unsatisfactory but greatly treasured twenty-minute fortnightly interview with my father. Mummy and I spent much time in the Ramakrishna Math. Sitting peacefully by the riverside, a new world of thought and experience opened out to me.

Soon afterwards, I joined Visva Bharati. Painfully shy with strangers, I was rather overawed by Gurudev's† magnificent presence. Never would I have dared to encroach upon his time, had he himself not complained of negligence. He kept close watch on all of us and seemed to be aware of all cross-currents in the institution. Many were the evenings when a small group of us sat at his feet and talked on diverse subjects, or silently watched him paint. Often he would recite or read aloud. These were moments of serene joy, memories to cherish.

My grandmother tried to get me engaged but this hazard was avoided thanks to Mummy's staunch support. Amongst other proposals of marriage came one from my husband and another from a stranger which had us laughing for days—but that is another story.

*Written in November 1959, for *Roshni*, journal of the All-India Women's Conference.
†The name by which Rabindranath Tagore was known.

3. A PAGE FROM THE BOOK OF MEMORY*

On the 9th August, 1942, the pre-dawn arrests of our leaders launched the Quit India Movement and I had my first experience of a tear gas attack at the flag-hoisting ceremony. My husband Feroze Gandhi decided to go underground, doing propaganda and other work. He grew a moustache and dressed in khaki. Because of his complexion, which was fair and ruddy, he passed off as an Anglo-Indian soldier. On his journey from Bombay he got off at a small wayside station, thinking that he was too well-known in Allahabad to risk being seen at the station, even in disguise. No conveyance was available and finally he hitched a ride from a truck full of British and Anglo-Indian soldiers, who were scared stiff and almost refused to let him get off again, saying that the damned natives would hack him to pieces if they found him alone and unarmed.

Swaraj Bhawan was occupied by the military, and next door in Anand Bhawan we had the unattractive sight of a row of guns aimed at us from across the garden wall. Our servants, mostly villagers, were naturally terrified and found it difficult to reply to the curt: "Halt, who goes there" every time they approached the wall.

There was a warrant for Shastriji's† arrest. Acting on the assumption that no one would ever guess that he could be rash enough to stay in Anand Bhawan, he did just that and remained with us incognito until he could make full arrangements for the work of the movement to go on. He could not come out of his room until after dark and food was taken up to him surreptitiously. We pretended we had an ailing relative. This situation could hardly be maintained for long without the news leaking out. Besides there was always the danger of a search; so Shastriji had to move and he did and was arrested within a short time. We were hedged in on all sides and it was well nigh impossible for workers to get together. My husband became one of the links through whom I could pass on money and political literature to other underground workers and we had to arrange to meet briefly and late at night in the houses of different non-political friends.

Then came information that I was to be arrested. Until then I had

*This article appeared in the journal *Women on the March*, September 1963.
†Lal Baharur Shastri, Prime Minister of India 1964–66.

tried to remain as inconspicuous as possible but I did not feel like going to jail so tamely. So I hastily packed some clothes and books and went to stay elsewhere. Whispered from ear to ear spread the news of a public meeting at five. Police swarmed all over the city for they could not discover the whereabouts of the meeting. At the scheduled time I emerged and crowds of people poured out from all sides, from the cinema house, the shops and nearby houses where they had been collecting for some hours. I had hardly spoken for ten minutes when truck-loads of armed British military drove up and formed a cordon around us. My husband had decided not to get involved and was looking down at us through the shutters of a first-floor window. However, at the sight of a gun barrel, just a yard away from my head, excitement and anxiety got the better of him and he came charging down, yelling at the sergeant to shoot or to lower his gun. The sergeant made the mistake of touching my arm to lead me to the prison van. It was like a signal, the crowd surged forth; my other arm was grabbed by some Congress women and I thought I would be torn asunder. Somehow we all survived. There was no firing, though rifle butts were used and many were hurt. A large number of us, men and women, including my husband and I were arrested. The ride to the jail was rather an extraordinary one, for the police in my van were apparently so moved by my talking to them that they apologised, put their turbans at my feet and wept their sorrow because of what their job compelled them to do!

Since earliest childhood I had visited jails either for trials of relations and friends or for unsatisfactory but highly-treasured twenty-minute interviews. People have heard of my parents' imprisonments but it is not often realised what a large number of relatives, on both my father's and mother's side—off-hand I can think of two dozen names but there were probably more—spent long years in prison. I do not know of any other family which was so involved in the freedom struggle and its hardships.

What a world of difference there is between hearing and seeing from the outside and the actual experience. No one who has not been in prison for any length of time can even visualise the numbness of spirit that can creep over one when, as Oscar Wilde writes—"each day is like a year, a year whose days are long." When day after day is wrapped in sameness and in spite and deliberate humiliation, Pethick-Lawrence said, "The essential fact in the life of the prisoner is that he takes on a sub-human status." Herded together like animals, devoid of dignity or privacy, debarred not only from outside company or news but from all beauty and colour, softness and grace. The ground, the walls, everything around us was mud-coloured and so became our jail-washed clothes; even our food tasted gritty. Through the barred apertures we were exposed to the dust storms, the monsoon downpour and the winter cold. Others had an interview and a letter once or twice a month but not me. My husband was in the same prison. After persistent efforts we were permitted a short interview but soon he was transferred to another town. I kept cheerful and busy, reading and teaching. I took over the entire care of a small baby whose mother I was coaching, to enable her to earn her living on her release.

There was no yearning for the outside world, for no one worthwhile was there. Besides, we had convinced ourselves that we were in for seven years. I was determined to bear all privations and insults smilingly. Many pictures come to mind: the visit of the Civil Surgeon sent by the Governor of the U.P., in view of the public concern over my ill-health. He prescribed a tonic and a special diet including delicacies such as Ovaltine. But hardly was his back turned when the Superintendent tore up the list and tossed the pieces on the floor. "If you think you are getting any of this," he said, "you are mistaken." This was surprising for I had not asked for anything—even the Surgeon's visit was unexpected.

One night we were startled out of sleep by a blood-curdling shriek. Although Zohra was the nastiest and most unpopular of our wardresses, we could sympathise with her terror and agitation, for there was an enormous cobra only a yard from our bars, coiled under one of the clocks which the wardress had to punch on her rounds. So, apart from the imminent danger of snake-bite there was the legitimate fear of losing her job. We were locked inside the barrack and she within the outer wall. There was no stick or other weapon. Zohra's shouts, now frightened, now exasperated, now bullying, now entreating, did nothing to shake the calm of the sentry outside, who wanted detailed information regarding the exact location of the snake, specifications of its length and breadth and so on. "*Are Kambakht!*" (O you unfortunate one) shouted Zohra. "Have I got a tailor's tape to measure it from head to tail?" It was several hours before the sentry could be persuaded to call the matron. Her house was three furlongs away and she in turn had to walk to the Superintendent's house to awaken him, before they could go together to the main office to fetch the key to the women's prison. By the time this little procession entered our enclosure, we had long since fallen asleep and the snake had glided away.

Another day, we barely escaped being burnt to death. It was wartime and the cantonment was crowded with not only British but Americans and Canadians as well. A Canadian ace pilot was struck by our Superintendent's attractive daughter. Once he was flying low over her house, as he often did, when his wing touched a telegraph wire and burst into flames. We saw it falling towards us at alarming speed but it just skirted the jail wall and crashed into a half-built bungalow not far away.

All things pass and so did this. My unexpected release was like coming suddenly out of a dark passage—I was dazzled with the rush of life, the many hues and textures, the scale of sounds and the range of ideas. Just to touch and listen was a disturbing experience and it took a while to get adjusted to normal living.

CHAPTER TWO

Gandhi and Nehru

1. MY REMINISCENCES OF "BAPU"*

IT IS DIFFICULT TO SAY WHEN I FIRST CAME INTO CONTACT WITH
Gandhi. He forms part of my earliest memories and as a very small child
I regarded him not as a great leader but more as an elder of the family to
whom I went with difficulties and problems which he treated with the
grave seriousness which was due to the large-eyed and solemn child I was.
Later, I disagreed with many of his ideas and had long discussions with
the usual dogmatism of the very young who think that they have all the
answers. It is only as one's experience and knowledge grow that the
widening of the horizon brings into view an unending vista of fields to
conquer and peaks beyond our reach or comprehension.

Even as I was thus arguing with him, I was amazed at his patience, his
interest in and awareness of the minutest details and the real pain he felt at
any wrongdoing.

As I grew up I learned to understand him better and to realise how intimately he was in contact with the masses of our country, their thoughts, their
ideals and aspirations. This contributed in no small measure to his greatness.

I came really close to him only towards the end, when in the aftermath
of Independence trainloads of refugees arrived from Pakistan with harrow-
ing tales of murder, rape and loot, which started off the nightmare of
retaliation in Delhi and Punjab. I had only been in Delhi a short time.
I had a tiny baby and was far from well, but Gandhi sent for me to work
in the terror-stricken Muslim areas of the city. It was dangerous work and

*Bapu was how Mohandas Karamchand Gandhi, the leader of the Indian freedom movement,
was called by his close followers. The word means "father". He was also referred to as Mahatma
or "man with a great soul". The Prime Minister's husband, Feroze Gandhi, was no relation of
Mahatma Gandhi.

This article was written in July 1957.

23

one calculated to bring the utmost unpopularity, and yet one could not say 'no' to the plea: "I trust you to see this work through. I have asked several others and they have replied 'Yes, Bapu', but I know they are still hesitating." For months I spent over twelve hours a day in the worst trouble spots. Whenever possible I went to Bapu to report and these visits gave me fresh strength; but on many days there just wasn't the time. On these occasions he would send a message or a flower. At last, peace reigned again in the narrowest *gali** and Hindu-Muslim neighbours were shaking hands and visiting one another's homes. I was exhausted and on the verge of collapse. Gandhi packed me off to Lucknow for a rest, with the wonderful words, "Now I know your education and your years abroad have not been wasted."

Gandhi always attempted to raise politics to a higher level and taught us that religion and politics were not theories to be expounded, but to be put into practice by making them part of our daily lives and of our normal thinking.

In India Gandhi is still a living force, because his personality is alive in our minds, and because Nehru is following a path based on Gandhi's basic ideals. As new problems arise, the path has to be widened to accommodate new answers rather than that the questions themselves be changed or confined to fit into a rigid pattern. I hope we will not stray from this path. Already in some quarters there is a tendency to lay stress only on the outer forms of Gandhism—*khadi*, prohibition, etc.—forgetting the fundamental thought of the man, his wide tolerance and his breadth of vision.

While Gandhi was with us, Gandhism, like all great religions in the lifetime of their founders, had a dynamic quality. It was living, growing and evolving. There was no set line to be followed, no question of interpretation. Each policy was formulated according to the circumstances. Gandhi's thoughts were seeped in religion and our old traditions and yet there was no narrowness in his beliefs or actions. He believed in the fundamental unity of all religions and said:

I do not want my house to be walled in on all sides and my windows to be stuffed. I want the cultures of all lands to be blown about my house as freely as possible, but I refuse to be blown off my feet by any of them. Mine is not a religion of the prison house, it has room for the least

*gali—lane.

among God's creations, but it is proof against the insolent pride of race, religion or colour.

The last time I met Gandhi was in January 1948, the day before his assassination. He sent a message telling us that he was free and would like us to come over. Just as I was getting into the car, our *mali** gave me a jasmine *veni*† for my hair. It was so fresh and fragrant that I did not use it but put it on Gandhi's bedside table. All the time we were talking, my son Rajiv, then three and a half years old, played with the flowers, decorating Gandhi. Sometimes he would slip the *veni*† on his feet like an anklet. Sometimes he would hang it on to his big toe. Bapu was in a remarkably relaxed mood and we talked of many things and of the film which we had seen the night before and to which he had not allowed his Asram girls to go. We had not found it a very pleasant experience and Gandhi told us that he had known what it would be like, because of the person who made it. He explained how each person was being subtly moulded and formed by his own thoughts and actions day by day and how these affected the quality of his work. He laughed and joked and was full of fun. Little did we guess that we would never see his wide toothless smile again, nor feel the glow of his protection.

His mission of guiding us to independence had been accomplished. He left us so suddenly that like the babes in the wood we felt alone and guideless in the forest of problems and difficulties. But his spirit was with us and a priceless legacy of faith, courage and determination to follow the path of duty and of service to the people of India which was so dear to his heart.

*mali—gardener; †veni—flowers threaded together.

2. MAHATMA GANDHI*

Each person's understanding of Gandhiji is a measure of his own change and growth. Whilst he was alive, many of my age group found it difficult to understand him. Some of us were impatient with what we considered to be his fads, and we found some of his formulations obscure. We took his Mahatmahood for granted, but quarrelled with him for bringing mysticism into politics.

This applied not only to my generation. In his autobiography my father

*This article was written for the centenary volume edited by Dr. S. Radhakrishnan, (1968).

describes the difficulty which he and others of his generation felt in integrating Gandhian ideas into their own thought structure. But little by little, the experience of the ebb and flow of our national movement enabled my father to arrive at a fuller understanding of Gandhiji and to weave the essential elements of Gandhiji's thinking into his own. He called him a "magician" and devotedly attempted to translate Gandhian thought into contemporary terms, to make it more comprehensible and to extend its influence to young people and intellectuals.

Gandhiji himself did not demand unquestioning obedience. He did not want acceptance of his ends and means without a full examination. He encouraged discussion. How many times have I not argued with him, even when a mere girl? He regarded no honest opinion as trivial and always found time for those who dissented from him—a quality rare in teachers in our country or in prophets anywhere. He was an untypical prophet also in that he did not lay claim to revelation. He held forth neither blandishment of reward nor fear of punishment. Nor was he weighed down by the burden of his mission. He was a saint who quipped and had use for laughter.

The centenary year of Gandhiji's birth also marks the fiftieth anniversary of the Jallianwala Bagh tragedy. Those who confuse rigidity or harshness with strength would do well to ponder over the far-reaching effects of this so-called stronghanded action on the future of the British Empire. Seldom has a single event so moved an entire nation, shocking it into a reappraisal of values and aims. It made a powerful impact on men like my grandfather and the poet Rabindranath Tagore. Tagore gave up his knighthood and wrote passionately and understandingly on the problems of colonialism. My grandfather, along with the entire family, was drawn into Gandhiji's circle. Our lives changed. The mood of the entire country changed. It was the year which brought Gandhiji to the helm of our political movement. Looking back on this half century, we are better able to realise the full impact of his personality and of his teaching, though a total assessment is still beyond us. We are too near to him, and still in a state of transition. Not for decades will we be able to wholly measure the extent of his work for India and for all mankind. Even so, one cannot but marvel at the turn Gandhiji gave to our history in that one year. It was as though with his two thin hands he lifted up a whole people. What changes he brought about in the personal lives of such a vast number of people, eminent and humble alike! To be the prime

mover of politics is not a greater achievement than to influence so profoundly the inner lives of people. Gandhiji differs from his fore-runners on
the national scene in that he rejected the politics of the elite and found the
key to mass action. He was a leader, closely in tune with the mass mind,
interpreting it and at the same time moulding it. "He was the crest of the
wave but they [the people] were the wave itself."

Gandhiji freed us from fear. The political liberation of the country
was not the culmination but a mere by-product of this liberation of the
spirit. Even more far-reaching was the alteration he brought about in the
sociological climate of India. Gandhiji set us free also from the walls and
fetters of our social tradition. It was his axiomatic assumption of the
equality of women and men, of the supposedly low-born and high-born,
the urban and the rural, that inducted the masses into the Gandhian
movement. In the long history of India, every reformer has fought
against the hierarchy of caste and the debasement of women but no one
succeeded in breaking down discrimination to the extent that Gandhiji
did. The women of India own him a special debt of gratitude. And so do
all other groups who suffered from age-old handicaps.

Mahatma Gandhi once wrote: "Let no one say that he is a follower of
Gandhi. It is enough that I should be my own follower. I know what an
inadequate follower I am of myself, for I cannot live up to the convictions
I stand for." The Gandhians would have us believe that Gandhiji evolved
a universal philosophy, analysing everything, reconciling everything and
prescribing for every contingency. How unfair this would be to a man
who never assumed omniscience and never stopped his experiments with
truth and understanding. He was an integrated being but he did not
deal in absolutes. Few men were greater idealists than he, but few more
practical. He propounded fundamental truths, but in every plan of action
that he drew up, he proceeded on the basis of "one step is enough for me".

The policy of planned industrial development which we have adopted
in the last two decades has sometimes been criticised as a calculated
abandonment of Gandhism. Those who level this charge and advocate
cottage industries do not themselves refrain from using the products of
large industry such as aircraft, automobiles and telephones. Gandhiji did
not shun the railways, and he was a punctilious user of watches. And if we
use railways and watches, does it make sense not to manufacture them
ourselves? Gandhiji's advocacy of cottage industries should therefore be
understood in the correct context. He was intensely concerned with

poverty. He abhorred waste. He wanted to use the latent energies of the vast army of rural unemployed to produce more goods for the nation and some wealth for themselves. Then again, like other sensitive men before him, he was reacting to the brutal effects of the first phase of industrialisation. As a seer concerned with the ultimate condition of man, he wanted to caution us against becoming prisoners of our own devices. In his copious writings on the place of the machine, there are many passages which show that Gandhiji's outlook was broader and more humanely practical than some literalist interpreters would have us believe.

To me Gandhiji is a living man who represents the highest level to which a human being can evolve. Seeped in the best from the past he lived in the present, yet for the future. Hence the timelessness of his highest thoughts. Much that he said and wrote was for the solution of immediate problems; some were for the inner guidance of individuals. His intellect did not feed on derived information. He fashioned his ideas as tools in the course of his experiments in the laboratory of his own life.

Speaking of Gandhiji's work in South Africa, Gopal Krishna Gokhale said that he made heroes out of clay. Sometimes I wonder whether we have not become clay again. The exaltation which a truly great teacher produces in his time cannot last very long. But the teaching and thought of such people have a reach farther than their own time and country. We who were born in Gandhiji's own time and country have a special obligation to cherish his image. More than his words, his life was his message.

It is not despite but through one's time and place that a man achieves true universality. Gandhiji identified himself totally with the common people of India. For this he even changed his mode of dress. Yet he was receptive to the best thought from other parts of the world. The impact of his days in England and South Africa as a student and practitioner of law was evident in his insistence on sanitation and in his habit of examining all that he heard by strictly applying the evidence act. But he assimilated everything he adopted and evolved Indian solutions to Indian problems.

Another of his glorious legacies is the secularism for which he gave his life. Secularism means neither irreligion nor indifference to religion, but equal respect for all religions—not mere tolerance, but positive respect. Secularism demands constant self-examination and unceasing exertion. That great truth is inscribed on rocks by Asoka, that no man reverences his own religion unless he reverences others' religion also. India has been great and has risen high in those periods when the truth was acknowledged and practised by her rulers. In our times Gandhiji and Jawaharlal Nehru made it a living reality for us. Without it there is no future for our nation.

I hesitate to speak of the other great teaching left us by Gandhiji, non-violence. I hesitate not because I find any justification for violence but because mankind has accumulated such a fearful store of weapons of destruction that I sometimes wonder whether we have any right to hope. Wars still erupt here and there, but even more distressing and alarming is the growth in all parts of the world of hatred in thought and violence in action, and the reckless recourse to the agitational approach. Gandhiji said: "In the midst of darkness, light persists." We must have faith. The ultimate justification of Gandhiji is that he showed how armed strength could be matched without arms. If this could happen once, can it not happen again?

Life means struggle and the higher you aim, the more you wish to achieve, the greater is the work and sacrifice demanded of you. Men of all religions have evoked the eternal truths. It is the great good fortune of India that she has given birth to great sons who have again and again revitalised her ancient thought to make it a part of the lives of the people. In our own lives, we were guided through perilous times by Mahatma Gandhi and Jawaharlal Nehru who merged themselves in the general good. Each complemented the other. Each taught that every decision should be put to the acid test of its relevance to the welfare of the multitude. More than any "ism", this guiding principle will save us from error. As my father said:

> ... the greatest prayer that we can offer is to take a pledge to dedicate ourselves to the truth, and to the cause for which this great countryman of ours lived and for which he has died.

3. JAWAHARLAL NEHRU: THE FOREWORD TO THE SELECTED WORKS

Jawaharlal Nehru is one of the key figures of the twentieth century. He symbolised some of the major forces which have transformed our age.

When Jawaharlal Nehru was young, history was still the privilege of the

West; the rest of the world lay in deliberate darkness. The impression given was that the vast continents of Asia and Africa existed merely to sustain their masters in Europe and North America. Jawaharlal Nehru's own education in Britain could be interpreted, in a sense, as an attempt to secure for him a place within the pale. His letters of the time are evidence of his sensitivity, his interest in science and international affairs as well as of his pride in India and Asia. But his personality was veiled by his shyness and a façade of nonchalance, and perhaps, outwardly there was not much to distinguish him from the ordinary run of men. Gradually there emerged the warm and universal being who became intensely involved with the problems of the poor and the oppressed in all lands. In doing so, Jawaharlal Nehru gave articulation and leadership to millions of people in his own country and in Asia and Africa.

That imperialism was a curse which should be lifted from the brows of men, that poverty was incompatible with civilisation, that nationalism should be poised on a sense of international community and that it was not sufficient to brood on these things when action was urgent and compelling—these were the principles which inspired and gave vitality to Jawaharlal Nehru's activities in the years of India's struggle for freedom and made him not only an intense nationalist but one of the leaders of humanism.

No particular ideological doctrine could claim Jawaharlal Nehru for its own. Long days in jail were spent in reading widely. He drew much from the thought of East and West and from the philosophies of the past and the present. Never religious in the formal sense, yet he had a deep love for the culture and tradition of his own land. Never a rigid Marxist, yet he was deeply influenced by that theory and was particularly impressed by what he saw in the Soviet Union on his first visit in 1927. However, he realised that the world was too complex, and man had too many facets, to be encompassed by any single or total explanation. He himself was a socialist with an abhorrence of regimentation and a democrat who was anxious to reconcile his faith in civil liberty with the necessity of mitigating economic and social wretchedness. His struggles, both within himself and with the outside world, to adjust such seeming contradictions are what make his life and work significant and fascinating.

As a leader of free India, Jawaharlal Nehru recognised that his country could neither stay out of the world nor divest itself of its own interests in world affairs. But to the extent that it was possible, Jawaharlal Nehru sought to speak objectively and to be a voice of sanity in the shrill phases of the "cold war". Whether his influence helped on certain occasions to maintain peace is for future historians to assess. What we do know is that for a long stretch of time he commanded an international audience reaching far beyond governments, that he spoke for ordinary, sensitive, thinking men and women around the globe and that his was a constituency which extended far beyond India.

So the story of Jawaharlal Nehru is that of a man who evolved, who grew in storm and stress till he became the representative of much that was noble in his time. It is the story of a generous and gracious human being who summed up in himself the resurgence of the "third world" as well as the humanism which transcends dogmas and is adapted to the contemporary context. His achievement, by its very nature and setting, was much greater than that of a Prime Minister. And it is with the conviction that the life of this man is of importance not only to scholars but to all, in India and elsewhere, who are interested in the valour and compassion of the human spirit that the Jawaharlal Nehru Memorial Fund has decided to publish a series of volumes consisting of all that is significant in what Jawaharlal Nehru spoke and wrote. There is, as is to be expected in the speeches and writings of a man so engrossed in affairs and gifted with expression, much that is ephemeral; this will be omitted. The official letters and memoranda will also not find place here. But it is planned to include everything else and the whole corpus should help to remind us of the quality and endeavour of one who was not only a leader of men and a lover of mankind, but a completely integrated human being.

4. JAWAHARLAL NEHRU: A TRIBUTE*

My father once said that to do justice to Gandhiji, one should be almost as great as Gandhiji himself. I think, perhaps, this is true of Jawaharlal Nehru himself and I certainly do not claim the ability to interpret his many-faceted personality. His spirit was so vital, his range of interests so wide and his work so varied, I do not know if we will ever know the man completely. Deliberate misunderstandings about him and his personality had been created during his lifetime by certain sections of our own people and these were taken up and exaggerated by foreign observers or

*Extempore remarks while releasing the first volume of the *Selected Works of Jawaharlal Nehru*.

experts, as they are sometimes called. But he remained throughout unshakable himself.

There are only two stories which come to mind just now. One was the famous "banyan tree". I personally think that nothing could have been more untrue about him because it was our constant complaint—especially mine and also of many young people and others—that he did allow everybody to grow—even those who should not be, even those whom we considered to be weeds, to put it frankly, and he did allow them to grow even though they were constantly threatening him. This was one story.

The other, of quite a different type, was about his wearing a Gandhi cap. Time and again, in almost every book about him I have read, it says that he wore a Gandhi cap because he looked more handsome in it. Now this is a matter of judgment. I know that when we were discussing the question of bringing out a stamp on him, I know that when various famous photographers wanted him to pose, the unanimous verdict was that he must take the cap off because of the beauty of his head. But in India, especially in North India, it is a mark of disrespect sometimes not to have your head covered and certainly during the Independence movement, the Gandhi cap had a particular association and it was worn as much for itself as a mark of defiance, a mark of assertion of what one believed in and what one was fighting for.

I have only mentioned these two very small points to show how something is picked up and it goes on pursuing you, no matter how much you try to shake it off.

Well, there are so many books about him. I do not think I have even seen half of them. But I am sure you will all agree that he was his own best biographer. It is not only his autobiography, *The Discovery of India*, and vast quantities of writings and speeches which reveal different aspects of a fascinating personality in which merged the personal, the national and the international, but his thoughts and his actions were so closely interwoven in the unfolding story of India and they provided much of its drama and influenced its trend. These are some of the reasons which prompted this compilation of an authentic record of Jawaharlal Nehru's writings and speeches.

Three of his books are famous and are perhaps the most authoritative guide to his thinking. But there is much more which is worth preserving and presenting for the benefit not only of the specialists and scholars but of the earnest citizen who would like to have a deeper understanding of his heritage. We were, by and large, a writing family. Each person among us, young or old, had his or her field of activity which kept us very busy. So the only way we could communicate, not necessarily a serious message but even some joy which we felt or some joke which we felt should be shared, was by putting it down in writing and leaving notes in various places where we hoped they would come to notice. And of course, because of his position and the type of work he undertook and later because of being Prime Minister naturally there was very much more to write about and the very quantity of what he produced is quite astounding.

Although the *Glimpses of World History* was especially written for me, I think I have felt closest to the *Discovery*, perhaps because I was entrusted with the reading of the proofs. And the very day the volume arrived from the publisher I came under an attack of the mumps. So, it is not an experience that I will easily forget. Mumps, as you know, is one of those illnesses which are hilarious to the person who comes and sees it but extremely painful for a person who has got it. So, I have very special memories of the early days of this book. The *Discovery* was completed in 1944 and he had twenty more years of crowded, creative life, record of which he kept in copious letters, speeches, documents and all of which are well-worth studying.

With the present Jawaharlal Nehru series, which is being published by the Memorial Fund, the approach is different. As Dr. Karan Singh has said just now, and as their titles indicate, they are selective and only such speeches and writings are included as will be of more than passing value.

Some very important and even historic documents will have to be left out because of reasons of official secrecy. It is estimated that the series will run into twenty volumes. Someone questioned the appropriateness of applying the word "selected" to such a bulky series. Had the yardstick been that of throwing light on current history much more would have to be included because from the literary and intellectual point of view so much of what he wrote was of extraordinary quality.

Most of you have heard of the fortnightly letters which he wrote to his ministerial colleagues and governors. He took great pains over them and they are a store-house of knowledge and wisdom on a variety of subjects. The official record shows these fortnightly letters add up to six thousand pages. That gives some idea of the material which exists. In eighteen years of office he naturally had to write a great deal of routine nature and many of his speeches were of necessity rather repetitive because he was an educator of the people. Through his speeches he reached out to the individual, regarding no one as too backward or too uneducated to understand national or international policies or even the intricacies of science and technology.

He was not just a fluent and a prodigious writer. He was meticulous and exacting. He believed in revising and checking what he wrote as is evident from the manuscripts of his books. This quality made the task of the editors very difficult. They had constantly to ask themselves what they could leave out in order to compress the material into twenty volumes.

We are fortunate in having as a General Editor a scholar and a historian of the calibre of Dr. Gopal. We are sorry he is not with us today because of a tragedy in his family.

I have great pleasure in releasing the first volume. I hope the series will prove a major contribution to the understanding of our times. Jawaharlal Nehru integrated our ideals into our national life laying the firm foundation of a secular democracy directed towards socialism. I think the greatest memorial to him is that today the people of India are forward-looking and self-confident.

CHAPTER THREE

Family Life

I. ON BEING A HOSTESS*

Situated as I am, it is perhaps inevitable that I should be asked a great many questions. But the most frequent is "How do you do it?" The answer lies in the great variety of my activities.

The social side, the political sphere, the welfare angle, the myriad activities connected with children, even the interest in folk-dance and art—all these have been laid bare to the public eye. Running through them and linking them together is the thread of domesticity. What a gentle word is domesticity. What form does it take when it involves my father, a being so versatile, at once volatile and calm, politician and poet, who finds himself equally at home in the richest palace or the poorest hut, who loves the jolting, the sweat and the tumult of immense crowds no less than the quietness and solitude of the Himalayas? I cannot even begin to describe it in the space of a short article. There can at best be only a glimpse here and a glimpse there.

Travelling around the world, meeting the first ladies of many lands, one is struck mostly by the similarity of the problems and difficulties facing the heads of government anywhere. For the women especially there is the constant battle with protocol. It is like walking on a tight rope to adhere close enough to the formal side of protocol so as not to offend even the most particular of dignitaries and yet manage not to stifle the human element and to keep the function interesting and homely, the daily struggle with menus to suit all tastes, the intricacies of decorating a State House, and so on.

Even such simple problems are made more complicated in India by the peculiar fads of our people. Apart from the main taboos of Hindus not

*This article was published in *The International*, sponsored by the International Club, Bombay, August 1957.

eating beef and Muslims not eating pork, there are endless combinations and permutations! There are meat-eaters who are vegetarians on certain days of the week—there are vegetarians who eat eggs, others eat fish as well, and one distinguished guest who declared himself a vegetarian, ended up by eating everything except chicken!

Even the quantity of food required differs. I had one experience which I had thought occurred only in nightmares! During our first year we had had several receptions at the in-between hour of 6.30 p.m. for diplomats and others, and had discovered that very little food was consumed. Then came a party for a slightly different crowd. On advice from the meteor- ological department the party had been arranged out of doors. Just as the guests were arriving there was a sudden thunderstorm and we had to herd them indoors, where it was so hot that a couple fainted off! When the food was shown around, instead of helping themselves to just one *samosa* or sweet, some of the guests relieved the bearers of the entire dish! To our mounting dismay and horror we saw the food being exhausted even before all the guests had arrived. That sturdy standby—the *pakora*—saved the day, along with dried fruit and nuts! Strange as it may seem neither my father nor the guests noticed anything out of the way. But since that dreadful day I take good care to have extra food available, and to make duplicate arrangements, outside and in, if there is even a speck of a cloud!

Happily nothing so unnerving has happened again. Through trial and error and with the help of a devoted and dedicated staff, even the strangest assignments are under control. Last year during the Buddhist conference we had arranged a lunch for the delegates which included the Dalai Lama and many venerable monks. Almost at the last moment we realised that the monks must eat their last meal before noon but that the other guests would not be free until 1.30. So we had seventy-five monks to lunch at 11.30 a.m. and a hundred others at 1.30. p.m.

Almost every time my father goes on a journey in India or abroad he finds recipes or customs of which he approves and which we have to adopt. The first time he dined at Buckingham Palace he decided that at our house too, milk and sugar should be poured before the coffee. This is often bewildering to our guests who look around furtively to see if they have somehow mislaid, or forgotten to take, the coffee.

On another trip he stayed at a country house and liked the idea of every- body serving himself at breakfast. This suited us fine, for each one of us has his activities and breakfast is a hurried meal. But again it is a habit to which guests could not accommodate themselves and it ended in our having to serve them ourselves.

The latest is rather a charming custom from Sweden. After every meal the children go up to their parents and thank them for the food. Rajiv and Sanjay still look very sweet and shy as they accomplish this unaccustomed rite.

Whatever other experiences we might share I wonder how many of these ladies have had to chase a panda through their living rooms or to sit up nights with a sick tiger?

When it was first decided that we would move into the then Commander-in-Chief's residence I came over to look at it and was at once plunged in gloom. Staring down from the walls of the public rooms were life-size portraits of stern generals, resplendent in their bemedalled uniforms. I felt they were watching every movement, criticising every unspoken thought. I could not be at ease until they were all taken down and hurriedly despatched to the Defence Ministry. Their removal made the rooms seem larger and the walls seemed to stretch in their stark bareness. Such enormous rooms, such long corridors: Could this ever be made livable, could it ever have any semblance to a home? I need not have worried. What house can resist fast-growing boys full of healthy noise and mischief and a host of animals?

We had always had dogs, the good kind with long pedigrees, and others rescued off the streets which were just as devoted—also parrots, pigeons, squirrels, and practically every small creature common to the Indian scene. And we thought life was pretty full, looking after them on top of all the other chores. Then in Assam, we were presented with a baby cat-bear (or red Himalayan panda), although we did not know what it was until we reached Agartala and were able to study the book of Indian animals in the Commissioner's library. The tribals had told us it was a kind of bear and expecting it to grow large and strong, the children decided to call it Bhimsa (like Bhim) even before they had seen the tiny ball of fur. We arranged a corner for Bhimsa in the children's bathroom but somehow I could not house-train him and he always climbed on to the towel-rack to do his business, besides racing all over the house. Finally we banished him to the garden—a large wire-netting enclosure was made with a little wooden house in a tree. And that is where he has lived ever since—except when he goes off to Naini Tal every summer. Much later we got him a mate, Pema (which means lotus in Tibetan), and now they have the most adorable little cubs—the first, I believe, to be born in captivity. My father calls on the panda family morning and evening. They miss him when he is out of station. Once when he was unwell we even took Bhimsa to call on him in his bedroom. The only things that make them unhappy are loud noises and the scent of the dogs and the tigers.

Two years ago we received our first tiger cubs—there were three named Bhim, Bhairav and Hidamba. A man came from the Lucknow Zoo to teach us how to look after them and advised us to have a cement floor in their enclosure. Unfortunately he put the cubs in before the cement had properly set, so that their paws were lacerated and infected. Two were cured with sulphur powder but little Bhim got worse and worse. Without our knowledge the vet in attendance decided to cauterise Bhim's paws, and, forgetting that despite his ferocious roar he was still a wee baby, gave him such a walloping doze of sedative that he practically collapsed. My father and I were terribly upset. After much telephoning we were lucky to contact another vet, who prescribed saline injections and constant watching night and day. One of our reception officers opted to stay half the night while I would go to bed at 10 p.m. and get up at 2 a.m. to take our duty. On the fifth morning Bhim raised his head. My own children had got used to playing with the cubs and did not care how boisterous they got, but for other children and visitors it was a boon to have Bhim still dazed and docile from his illness, and many who ordinarily would not come within ten yards felt courageous enough to stroke him! He recovered fast and only too soon was too big to be kept in the open in a house which had so much *va et vient*. Reluctantly we sent them off to the Lucknow Zoo, where you can still meet Bhim and Hidamba; magnificent beasts, their muscles rippling with power and grace. While they were with us they were petted by many distinguished people including Marshal Tito and U Nu. The Marshal asked for one of them and Bhairav now resides in Belgrade.

There are golden moments too. I love birds and mountains and music and pictures and yet all these cannot vie with the deep joy of bringing some small measure of happiness to a human being.

During the partition riots I had saved many lives, only alas to earn the worst abuse from the victims as well as the attackers. For months afterwards streams of refugees used to pour in. Everyday I sat solidly and patiently in one place between 8 a.m. and 1.30 p.m. and sometimes again in the afternoons interviewing group after group. For the majority there was not much one could do except listen to their tale of woe, but even this apparently gave peace of mind and there were always just enough cases which were within one's power to help to keep up hope. Along with this mêlée came Satya, about twenty years old, daughter of a murdered railway level crossing watchman. As a child she was run over and lost both legs at thigh level. The only movement possible was by dragging herself on her hands, consequently her body had become mis-shapen. It was a distressing sight. There was no way of really helping her except by providing artificial legs and this I resolved to do.

It was no easy task to discover first that the Artificial Limb Centre, Poona, catering exclusively for the armed forces, was the only institution in India capable of this service; secondly it took me months to persuade the then Defence Minister, Sardar Baldev Singh, to make an exception and to allow Satya to be admitted into the institution (this precedent plus further effort later on succeeded in permanently opening the doors of the institution to civilians). Several visits to Poona were required and many painful months of patient endurance which were interspersed with fits of depression—dark moments when she felt it wasn't worthwhile to persevere and when she sought me out for reassurance. At last her body had been coaxed into normal shape and she was not only fitted with the final pair of legs but had learned to use them with the greatest self-assurance. She came to show off a little and to announce her engagement, her face transformed, glowing, positively scattering the gold dust of her happiness on all who happened to be near.

Every now and then when I seem to be going around in circles, when my efforts seem so feeble compared with the immensity of the task, the memory of Satya's radiance, like Wordsworth and his daffodils, comes to mind and I cannot help myself smiling.

Have I, in this random meandering, answered the question "How?", or have I merely provoked another one "When"?

2. ON BEING A MOTHER

Tagore wrote, "Every child comes with the message that God is not discouraged of man." But to a woman, motherhood is the highest fulfilment. To bring a new being into this world, to see its tiny perfection and to dream of its future greatness is the most moving of all experiences and fills one with wonder and exaltation.

Because of the political struggle my own childhood was an abnormal one, full of loneliness and insecurity. That is why I was determined to devote full time to my children. However, life does not run according to our desires or expectations and when India became free, I was catapulted into a new life and involved in new responsibilities which have grown considerably with the years. At first it was only a question of setting up a home for my father in New Delhi and coping with the social obligations of the Prime Minister's House. But gradually, circumstances and my own intense interest in the path which the country was trying to follow, drew me deeper into public affairs.

A child's need of a mother's love and care is as urgent and fundamental as that of a plant for sunshine and water. To a mother, her children must always come first because they depend on her in a very special way. The main problem in my life was, therefore, how to reconcile my public obligations with my responsibility towards my home and my children.

When Rajiv and Sanjay were babies I did not like the idea of anyone else attending to their needs and tried to do as much for them as I could. Later when they began school, I took care to have my engagements during school hours so as to be free when the boys returned home. Once when Sanjay was quite small, a nursery school friend of his came to our house with his mother. The mother, a society lady of means, commenting on my public work remarked that I could not be spending much time with my sons. This hurt Sanjay and before I could think of a reply he rushed to my rescue with the words—"My mother does lots of important work yet she plays with me more than you do with your little boy." It seemed his little friend complained about his mother's bridge playing.

However, it is not the amount of time spent with the children that matters as much as the manner of spending it. When one has only a limited period at one's command, one naturally makes the most of it. No matter how busy I have been, or how tired or even unwell, I have taken time off to play or read with my sons.

One can teach best by example. Children are extraordinarily perceptive and quick to detect any falsehood or pretence. If they trust and respect you, they will co-operate with you even at a very young age. My elder son Rajiv had been a happy laughing baby but at the age of three, the advent of a baby brother coinciding with our move from the familiar Allahabad atmosphere and many other changes temporarily upset him. I was far from well and I found his tantrums very irritating. Scolding only made it worse. So I tried reasoning. I told him that much as I loved him, his shouting disturbed me. "What can I do?" he said, "I don't want to cry, it just comes." I said, "There is a nice fountain in our garden. When you want to cry or shout, go to the fountain and do it there." After that at the first signs of tears, I would whisper "fountain" and away he went. In the garden there was much to distract his attention and he soon forgot his troubles.

When the boys grew older, they went to boarding school. That is when I began touring the country. I would travel extensively while they were away, so as to be with them during the vacations. Whenever I was separated from the boys, I wrote to them at least once a week and sometimes more often, so that they would know that I was thinking of them.

Life is a mixture of happiness and sorrow. Education in the widest sense of the word is the training of the mind and body, so as to produce a balanced personality which is capable of adjusting, without undue disturbance, to life's changing situations. This cannot be achieved through schools or book knowledge alone. Much of the burden falls on the mother, who must help the child to develop self-discipline and strengthen his character. Real love is not that which gives in to the child's whims but which can also discipline and teach whenever necessary.

When Rajiv was under 12 years old, he had to have an operation. The surgeon wanted to tell him that it would not hurt but in my opinion this would have been an insult to the child's intelligence, so I interrupted to inform Rajiv that there would be considerable pain and discomfort for a few days after the operation. Had it been possible for me to take on his suffering I should gladly have done so but since this was not possible he must be prepared to endure it. Weeping or complaining would make no difference except perhaps to produce a headache as well. Rajiv never once cried out or complained but bore the pains smilingly. The doctor said he had never had such a good patient even among older people.

My public work has sometimes taken me away from the children. Yet even they feel it is worthwhile because through it I am attempting to play my part in building a better future for all the children of India.

3. INDIA TODAY

You have asked me to speak on India today.* My father once said, "To endeavour to understand and describe the India of today would be the task of a brave man." I hope I am not lacking in courage, but I doubt if courage alone will take me far in this respect. Time is just as important and we are short on time. I shall have to confine myself to only a few aspects of the India of today. And herein lies my difficulty. What aspects would interest you the most? It is not easy for a stranger to judge.

However, there are certain basic facts which are an essential background to any picture one may wish to paint. India is a sub-continent. India is a land of contradictions. You must have heard these clichés a hundred times, but one cannot avoid them. The problems of India have to be viewed in the context of her vast size, of the enormous diversity of her culture, languages, customs and so on, as well as a basic underlying unity which has persisted through the ages. We must also keep in view historical influences and the strong attachment to tradition.

Let us look at pre-Independence India. Politically, she was a colony with all the complexes, frustrations and warping of the personality which subjugation involves. Economically, she who had so long been renowned for her wealth and riches, was now helping to advance the industrial power of her rulers while she herself sank into poverty—abject, abysmal and unbelievable poverty. The land could no longer support the increasing population, but there was no other outlet for work or employment. Social conditions were stagnant, for our rulers did not wish to offend orthodox elements and discouraged social reforms. Culturally, her heritage, which was so rich and remarkable and which had nurtured her people through thousands of years, was in disrepute. Her craftsmen were losing their skill and the people their self-respect. The old Indian systems of education and medicine had died out. Western systems reached only a handful. These were some of the darkest years in India's long history.

The struggle for political independence was long and hard and alongside it were powerful movements for social reform. Our movement for freedom was unique, not only because it was on a mass scale involving the

*This speech was given at the Women's National Press Club in Washington on November 7, 1961.

lowliest peasant and worker along with intellectuals and even people in the British Services, but because, with a few exceptions, success was achieved entirely by non-violent methods.

The Indian National Congress which was responsible for the attainment of Independence, was fully aware of the vastness of the tasks which freedom would bring and that the main and overwhelming problem was that of poverty and unemployment. The Party realised that we could only begin to tackle this problem by careful and long-term planning. The essence of planning is to find a way to utilise all available resources—of manpower, money, etc., and not to leave these things more or less to chance. Our aim was rapid economic growth and expansion of employment, reduction of disparities in income and wealth, prevention of concentration of economic power and the creation of the values and attitudes of a free and equal society. These are vital objectives. Where the bulk of the people live so close to the margin of poverty, the claims of social justice, of the right to work, of equal opportunity and a minimum level of living have great urgency.

Considering the extremely difficult period, the upheaval caused by the partition of the country, various natural calamities such as the severest earthquakes we have ever known, to say nothing of floods, drought, etc., it is quite astonishing how much we have been able to accomplish. I do not wish to bore you with figures, but a few may interest you. During the ten years of planning, our national income has shown a rise of 42 per cent and per capita income 16 per cent, food-grain production 46 per cent. The most important of all, steel production has been more than doubled—an increase of 120 per cent—and iron ore 234 per cent. The number of students as well as schools has doubled and expansion has taken place in the construction of hospitals, railways, roads, irrigation and power, etc.

We have a democratic system of government. There are many types of democracies in the world. But I think you will agree that some are more democratic than others and if you have been in India, I am sure you will also agree that India will find a place amongst the most democratic. Many people feel that had we not insisted on democracy, we could have progressed faster. Obviously, it is easier to order than to persuade and we deliberately chose the more difficult path in the belief that it was the surer and better one and that it would educate and strengthen the people towards fuller political maturity. The jump from a bullock-cart to a jet-plane is not more dramatic than that of a feudal society to a modern

democratic one. It is not easy for a largely illiterate public fully to appreciate the abstract ideal of democracy. Nor could one vote in five years
evoke an atmosphere of participation in the running of the nation's
affairs. So we have revived the ancient system of Panchayats (village
governments by an elected panel of villagers) and given it authority
and resources. Thus the villager can witness the day-to-day working of
democracy in his own village and can understand that Parliament is more
or less the same thing on a much vaster scale. In one village in South
India, because of quarrels amongst the men, the village decided to elect
only women.

Our Ambassador, Mr. B. K. Nehru, cabled to me that the Women's
Press Club was protesting against treating them or me merely as women
and that I should speak about social, economic and political developments
in India. But I feel that no picture of India can be complete without a word
about its women.

It is remarkable that in India, in every age, there have been women who
have had the strength of character to distinguish themselves in public
activities. Our history is rich in the names of women of wisdom and courage and talent. Indian women became famous in different spheres of life;
political, cultural, literary and religious. Amongst the names that have
come down to us, there are renowned scholars, a brilliant mathematician
and an astronomer of note. There were saints and poets, queens who are
still quoted as symbols of good government, and others who led their
armies into battle. One of the best loved and bravest of these was Lak-
shmibai, Rani of Jhansi, who won the highest praise even from the British
General whom she fought. However, until a few years ago, our women
were burdened with the most unjust social laws and customs. Women's
movements developed along with the struggle for freedom and the urge
for social reform. It was left to our political party and the wisdom of its
leader, Mahatma Gandhi, to persuade and encourage women, at all levels
of society, to leave the seclusion of their homes and to take part in the
most difficult tasks of the freedom struggle. This policy has been continued
by the leaders of the Congress Party in India and, under the Constitution,
our women have equal rights. An increasing number of them are now
participating in every sphere of public life and activity. New laws attempt
as a whole to reinterpret the ancient laws in terms of modern trends.

We have women Governors, women Ministers and Ambassadors.
Women occupy high posts in the administrative, judicial, educational

and medical services. They are active in business concerns. The Indian National Congress had had three women presidents before Independence. During the last election, the Congress Party attempted to nominate women for fifteen per cent of the candidates selected. We have now 49 women Members of Parliament out of a total of 700 in both Houses. There are 205 women amongst the 2908 members of the State Legislatures. Even so, women have a long way to go. We are not so interested in some women attaining high positions as in raising the status of the average woman. Much has to be done to arouse public consciousness. In the next few years, the proportion of girls should increase since 1750 million rupees have been especially allotted for the development of girls' education and the providing of facilities to persuade parents to send their daughters to school.

We are over-populated and the population is increasing. This is not due to a big increase in the birth-rate, which actually has gone down from 4·17 per cent in 1951–56 to 3·9 per cent in 1956–61, but because of improved health services, longer life expectancy and the decrease of infant mortality. In the forties the expectation of life was under 30; now it is 47½.

India is one of the few countries where family planning is part of the Government's policy. While progress is still slow, we feel that a foundation has been laid and work should now proceed at a faster rate. The outlay in the Third Plan for this purpose is 500 million rupees and we hope to have 8,200 clinics, out of which over 6,000 will be in the rural areas. In addition to these clinics, family planning services are provided at thousands of rural and urban medical and health centres.

India is one of the few, or perhaps even the only country in the world, where the people's links with their ancient culture and traditions have been maintained through thousands of years. There have been many invasions but each successive wave of a foreign culture has been absorbed and has become part of Indian culture. Our culture therefore is a composite one and, thanks to the wisdom of our ancient sages and wise men, there is cultural unity throughout the country and a basic quality of Indianness which persists in spite of many superficial differences. We have fourteen national languages, each with an ancient literature, drama, poetry, etc. There is infinite variety in costumes, dances, customs and so on. It was only the latest occupation, the British one, which did not adopt India as its home and which resulted in the suppression, directly and indirectly, of every aspect of our culture. It was this suppression which gave the impetus for a determined spirit of nationalism and also for the fierce regional and linguistic pride which culminated in the demand for linguistic States and which is today creating thorny problems for us. However, many of these problems are passing phases and can be solved. I believe that the strong cultural bonds, along with the economic dependence of one region on another, will keep us united.

The Unesco Constitution states that "War begins in the minds of men." So does everything else. To catch up with the more economically advanced nations, India needs a complete reorientation of her thinking. It is not enough to pass social legislation, the public must recognise the need for it and be willing to implement it. It is not enough to have scientific and technical institutions, the public itself must become scientific and technical minded. To change the minds of men, to put in one set of ideas instead of another, is difficult enough, but we are aiming beyond this. We want to open the doors and windows into minds which have been conditioned by centuries of tradition and conformity, which have become unaccustomed to new ideas and shun all innovation. We are attempting to train the people to think for themselves. This is the big and the most important revolution which is taking place in the minds of the Indian people. Professor Kabir writes, "The ferment that characterises much of India's life today is evidence of her efforts to assimilate new forces which contact with the West has brought." Here again we are forging a new path for ourselves by attempting to evolve a way of life which will embrace the best of both worlds. Material welfare is essential to man, but it is not sufficient for his total needs. The wisdom of our ancient scriptures is timeless, for it stresses the dignity of the individual, the many-sidednesses of truth and teaches tolerance, and understanding of differing viewpoints, and the acceptance of change as a way of life.

CHAPTER FOUR

Speeches, 1966–1970

1. BROADCAST TO THE NATION*

THIRTY-SIX YEARS AGO, ON THIS VERY DAY, MY VOICE WAS ONE of thousands repeating the historic and soul-stirring words of our Pledge of Independence.

In 1947 that pledge was fulfilled. The world knew that a new progressive force, based on democracy and secularism, had emerged. In the seventeen years that Jawaharlal Nehru was Prime Minister, the unity of this country with its diversity of religion, community and language became a reality, democracy was born and grew roots. We took the first steps towards securing a better life for our people by planned economic development. India's voice was always raised in the cause of the liberation of oppressed peoples, bringing hope and courage to many. It was heard beyond her frontiers as the voice of peace and reason, promoting friendship and harmony amongst nations.

During his brief but memorable stewardship, Shastriji enriched the Indian tradition in his own way. He has left our country united and determined to pursue our national objectives. Only yesterday we committed his mortal remains to the sacred rivers. The entire country sorrowed for the great loss. I feel his absence intensely and personally, for I worked closely with him for many years.

My own approach to the vast problems which confront us is one of humility. The tradition left by Gandhiji and my father, and my own unbounded faith in the people of India give me strength and confidence. Time and again, India has given evidence of an indomitable spirit. In recent years, as in the past, she has shown unmistakable courage and capacity for meeting new challenges. There is a firm base of Indianness, which will withstand any trial.

*Broadcast two days after becoming Prime Minister on January 26, 1966.

The coming months bristle with difficulties. We have numerous problems requiring urgent action. The rains have failed us. There has been drought in many parts. As a result, agricultural production, which is still precariously dependent on weather and rainfall, has suffered a sharp decline. Economic aid from abroad and earnings from export have not come to us in the measure expected. The lack of foreign exchange has hurt industrial production. Let us not be dismayed or discouraged by these unforeseen difficulties. Let us face them boldly. Let us learn from our mistakes and resolve not to let them recur. I hope to talk to you from time to time to explain the measures we take and to seek your support for them.

Above all else we must ensure food to our people in this year of scarcity. This is the first duty of Government. We shall give urgent attention to the management and equitable distribution of foodgrains, both imported and procured at home. We expect full co-operation from State Governments and all sections of the people in implementing our plans for rationing, procurement and distribution. Areas like Kerala which are experiencing acute shortage will receive particular attention. We shall try especially to meet the nutritional needs of mothers and children in the scarcity-affected areas to prevent permanent damage. We cannot afford to take risks where basic food is concerned. We propose, therefore, to import large enough quantities of foodgrains to bridge this gap. We are grateful to the United States for her sympathetic understanding and prompt help.

Only greater production will solve our food problem. We have now a well-thought-out plan to reach water and chemical fertilisers and new high-yielding varieties of seed as well as technical advice and credit to farmers. Nowhere is self-reliance more urgent than in agriculture, and it means higher production not only for meeting the domestic needs of a large and increasing population, but also for growing more for exports. We have to devise more dynamic ways of drawing upon the time and energy of our rural people and engaging them in tasks of construction. We must breathe new life into the rural works programme and see that the income of the rural labourer is increased.

Our strategy of economic advance assigns a prominent role in the public sector for the rapid expansion of basic industries, power and transport. In our circumstances, this is not only desirable but necessary. It also imposes an obligation to initiate, to construct and manage public sector enterprises for further investments. Within the framework of our plans, there is no conflict between the public and private sectors. In our mixed economy, private enterprise has flourished and has received help and support from Government. We shall continue to encourage and assist it.

Recent events have compelled us to explore the fullest possibilities of technological self-reliance, how to replace, from domestic sources, the materials we import, the engineering services we purchase, and the know-how we acquire from abroad. Our progress is linked with our ability to invent, improvise, adapt and conserve. We have a reservoir of talented scientists, engineers and technicians. We must make better use of them. Given the opportunity, our scientists and engineers have demonstrated their capacity to achieve outstanding results. There is the shining example of Dr. Homi Bhabha and the achievements of the Atomic Energy Establishment. The path shown by Dr. Bhabha will remain an inspiration.

Our programmes of economic and social development are encompassed in our plans. The Third Five Year Plan is drawing to a close. We are on the threshold of the Fourth. The size and content of the Fourth Plan received general endorsement of the National Development Council last September, even while we were preoccupied with the defence of our country. Its detailed formulation was interrupted due to many uncertainties, including that of foreign aid. We propose now to expedite this work. In the meantime an annual plan has been drawn up for 1966–67, the first year of the Fourth Plan, which takes into account the main elements of the Five Year Plan.

In economic development, as in other fields of national activity, there is a disconcerting gap between intention and action. To bridge this gap we should boldly adopt whatever far-reaching changes in administration may be found necessary. We must introduce new organisational patterns and modern tools and techniques of management and administration. We shall instil into the governmental machinery greater efficiency and a sense of urgency and make it more responsive to the needs of the people.

In keeping with our heritage, we have followed a policy of peace and friendship with all nations, yet reserved to ourselves the right to independent opinion. The principles which have guided our foreign policy are in keeping with the best traditions of our country, and are wholly consistent with our national interest, honour and dignity. They continue to remain valid. During my travels abroad I have had the privilege of meeting leaders in Government and outside and have always found friendship and an appreciation of our stand. The fundamental principles laid down by my father, to which he and Shastriji dedicated their lives, will continue to guide us. It will be my sincere endeavour to work for the strengthening of peace and international co-operation so that people in all lands live in equality, free from domination and fear.

We seek to maintain the friendliest relations with our neighbours and to resolve any disputes peacefully.

Peace is our aim but I am keenly aware of the responsibility of government to preserve the freedom and territorial integrity of the country. We must therefore be alert and keep constant vigil, strengthening our defences as necessary. The valour, the determination, the courage and sacrifice of our fighting forces have set a shining example. My thoughts go out today to the disabled and the families of those who gave their lives.

Peace we want because there is another war to fight—the war against poverty, disease and ignorance. We have promises to keep to our people— of work, food, clothing and shelter, health and education. The weaker and underprivileged sections of our people—all those who require special measures of social security—have always been and will remain uppermost in my mind.

Youth must have greater opportunity. The young people of India must recognise that they will get from their country tomorrow what they give her today. The nation expects them to aspire and to excel. The worlds of science and art, of thought and action beckon to them. There are new frontiers to cross, new horizons to reach and new goals to achieve.

No matter what our religion, language or State, we are one nation and one people. Let us all, farmers and workers, teachers and students, scientists and technologists, industrialists, businessmen, politicians and public servants, put forth our best effort. Let us be strong, tolerant and disciplined, for tolerance and discipline are the very foundations of democracy. The dynamic and progressive society, the just social order which we wish to create, can be achieved only with unity of purpose and through hard work and co-operation.

Today I pledge myself anew to the ideals of the builders of our nation— to democracy and secularism, to planned economic and social advance, to peace and friendship among nations.

2. ADDRESS AT MADRAS UNIVERSITY, 1967

I was wondering what I should speak about. But the theme has been given to me by my friends upstairs who have raised slogans. What is the problem before the nation today? The problem is to build, not to break, to construct and to raise, not to bring down. And this is what we expect from our universities and from our students who have the very great privilege of having an education.

We are at the most critical stage in our development. Sitting here on the platform, I was looking at your magazine, and at a quotation from *Alice in Wonderland.* I remembered another incident in the same book. This girl Alice comes across one of the queens, who is running very hard and Alice asks the queen "Why are you running so hard?" She says "Well, I have to run to stay in the same place." India is very much in that position today.

The advance of science and technology has helped mankind to go ahead. But they are helping those people who already have more. That seems to be the law of life. To those who have, more shall be given. Also, the more you have, the easier it is to gain more. Suppose you have a library and you have the best books in the library and you make the library free for everyone to use. Who will benefit? Only those who can already read, who already have an education. A person who cannot read, even though given full opportunity to use the library, will not be able to benefit from it. The same thing is happening with science and technology.

Many of our problems in the country are problems which are inherent in development and growth. We are in a state of transition. A colonial country has become free. A feudal society is trying to modernise itself. Many things are happening at the same time. The change has been abrupt. Whenever there is a change there is conflict. There is obstruction from those who do not wish to change. Some do not want change because they would lose what they have, but many more because they feel safer with what is familiar. But young people are for change because they look to the future. They who can help to bring about these changes have a stake in the future. It is heartening to know that through these Planning

Forums medical students are treating people in villages and other kinds of work have been taken up. As you all know, Uttar Pradesh in the north is going through an extremely difficult situation because of an unprecedented drought for the third consecutive year. There the students of one particular district, the Gorakhpur district, decided that they would help the people. Students and teachers of colleges and schools have gone out into the fields and have dug a large number of wells. I welcome this spirit of building, of trying to face difficulty and of refusing to be crushed.

We have demands which we cannot fulfil. Every country has been through some such phase. But there is a difference between the advanced countries and ourselves. Take England, a country with which we were very closely connected. They had the same sort of feudal stiuation as we had—that is, a few rich people and a large number of poor people with no education and no opportunities. Then the growth of knowledge brought about the Industrial Revolution. In the beginning the few rich people were able to exploit labour in order to build up industry. There was no political consciousness. So they could use the poor—men, women and even small children. If you have read your Dickens, then you would have known about children working twelve hours a day, never seeing the sun and dying very young. In such conditions, and with the help that she had from her colonies, England was able to industrialise herself. Up to that time there was no mass education. Education was only for a very few selected families. But when the Industrial Revolution was in progress, the need arose for more skilled workers to manage complicated machinery. So it was felt that the people should be educated. So came education, and with education came the consciousness of rights, of equality, fraternity and liberty. These we take for granted today, but they are really of very recent history. In England the desire for liberty and equality and the demands for better education and better living conditions arose after the industrial base was already there, and the demands could therefore be met. What has happened in India is the opposite. We were a slave country. So first came political consciousness. After that came large-scale education. These were followed by demands for the many things that we have been so long without. But we cannot have them immediately, because the Industrial Revolution which could have produced the good things that the people are asking for is far from being complete. This is a circumstance which history has created. The question today is: What do we do? Do we just sit and say that things are very difficult, things have gone wrong, and nothing can be put right? Or do we take a constructive attitude—not the "Down Down" attitude but, if I may say so, the "Up Up" attitude.*

All of us need to have certain basic necessities. Over and above them we have other needs. The more educated we are the more are our needs and the more we can advance. But the question arises: How much should we take when we know that so many others are deprived? This is a question to which there is no easy answer. We cannot say: Let us cut off higher learning because many people are not in school. If we did that it would be bad for administration. There would be a big gap in building up an intelligentsia which is equally important for a country's progress.

Today we have to get rid of those two ancient weaknesses which, in my view, first got us into this spot. We must have unity. It is because of its lack that we fell a prey to foreign power. This is where language comes in, to some extent. How do we have unity if we cannot communicate? I happen to know a little bit of the English language, and you know it, and so I can communicate with you. But if I go to a village in Madras I cannot communicate with anybody. And if I come all the way to Madras the loss is mine: here I am, but I am not able to learn anything about this place, or about the people who are my people and to whom I feel just as close as to people anywhere else. So this is a big loss. Also, once you are a scientist or take to some other profession, it is not good enough if you are confined to Madras. You have to know what other people in your line are doing in other parts of the country. You have to know what people in your line are doing in other parts of the world, and that is why I am not against English. In fact, I feel that English is a language we cannot afford to lose, it is our window, it is our link with the outside world. And if we were to lose it then we would go back to that old state of saying, "Well, this is India and here I stay, I don't take anything from outside." That is a weakening thing and it has weakened us in two ways. Not only did we get nothing from outside but we could not give to other people what we valued.

I am all for modernisation. I believe that it is absolutely essential for our country that young people should spearhead the modernising of our country. By that I mean not just copying certain western methods but trying to have a more scientific and rational outlook on life, fighting all

*The reference is to the "Down with Hindi" slogans shouted at the beginning of the meeting.

those things which have come down to us through the centuries which are now outmoded and have no place in a modern society. But I don't think I am against tradition as such. I believe that our ancient tradition, our ancient philosophy, has much in it that is timeless, that is of the same value today as it was thousands of years ago and will be perhaps a thousand years hence. These timeless values and ideas we must stick to. They are our roots. They are our strength. But over the centuries, over the years, if you don't keep cleaning any place it gathers dust and cobwebs. No matter how beautiful a house you build, how beautiful a temple you build, if you don't keep cleaning it, it will gather dust and soon nobody will be able to see whether it is beautiful or not, because of the dirt. So in society also you have to have this constant cleaning. There are things that suit the conditions of a point of time. There is no point in sticking to them even though the conditions have changed. It needs a great deal of courage to stand up against familiar customs and to want to root them out.

Already a very visible change has taken place, even amongst farmers. Some years ago if you went to a farm and if a person like me talked about agriculture, they would just say, "What do you know about agriculture? You live in a city. Our grandfathers, our great-grandfathers, have tilled the field. We know what to do." But today they will take instruction from you. If they consider it a practical method, they are willing to take the risk of trying it out. This is a tremendous advance for such a conservative society as ours. This revolution in the thinking of people is very real. Yet it is not fast enough. We are still embedded in all kinds of superstitions and in all kinds of thinking which prevents us from taking any step forward.

Whenever you take a step forward you are bound to disturb something. You disturb the air as you go forward, you distrurb the dust, the ground. You trample upon things. When a whole society moves forward this trampling is on a much bigger scale and each thing that you disturb, each vested interest which you want to remove, stands as an obstacle. This is where the young people must show courage.

When Winston Churchill was asked which was the most important virtue, he thought a great deal and he said finally, "Courage." Without courage you cannot practise any other virtue. You have to have courage—courage of different kinds. First, intellectual courage, to sort out different values and make up your mind about which is the one which is right for you to follow. You have to have moral courage then to stick to that—no matter what comes in your way, no matter what the obstacle and the opposition is. Opposition comes not only from your enemies but sometimes from your friends and the latter is much more difficult to face. You have to have physical courage, because very often going along the path of your choice is full of physical hardship.

I shall give an instance from our independence struggle. Can you imagine a time when an Indian in his own country, in his own city, was not allowed to walk along the main street? I don't know conditions in Madras but I do know cities in U.P. where such was the condition that an Indian, even if he had the money, could not travel in a first-class railway compartment. It was reserved for Englishmen. Looking back now it is very easy to say: What was the difficulty? All you had to do is to say, "I will travel first class." But for the first few people, it required real courage to do it, courage of all the three kinds I mentioned. Not only intellectual and moral courage, but physical courage also, because quite often they were just picked up and thrown out on the platform. Here I come to the personal story that I promised to give. It happened to my grandfather. He was one of those pioneers who tried to break through obstacles. As you know he was a self-made man. He made a great deal of money. He lived very comfortably. He had many English friends. And because of his friendship with many important Englishmen he could travel where he liked and he could do what he liked. But he felt that it was not a question of his travelling but of any Indian travelling. It was not a question of his being able to do something but of every Indian being able to do it, if he so desired.

We have a hill station in the U.P. called Naini Tal with a very beautiful lake, where no Indian was allowed to swim or sail. My grandfather said, "Well, I am going to sail here." For some days he was fined fifty rupees every day. And believe me, in those days fifty rupees was supposed to be a very large sum. But he said: "Even if I am bankrupt I am going to do this everyday till everybody gets used to seeing an Indian on the lake and will say, why cannot an Indian sail?" That was what happened. For one whole season he kept on paying the fine and being handled back from the lake and the next season everybody said, "Well, this is too much trouble. If he wants to sail let him sail." And of course when he sailed other people also could do it. This as a very small thing. It is not at all important whether you do sail or you don't. But I am giving it as an example of how you have to fight even on small things in order to attain the bigger things.

When my grandfather was once thrown out from a first-class compartment, he decided that he must do something, and find a way by which he was not thrown out. In those days hardly anybody travelled alone, as you know. Not only did they travel with their retinue but they took a mountain of luggage, because everything that one needed, bedding, cooking utensils, everything had to go from home. My grandfather used to take with him two very tall and broad nephews—I suppose as his bodyguards. What actually happened was that there he would be sitting in his compartment or standing outside it, and some English people would come in and say, "Here is a compartment nearly empty", and they would look at him and say, "Oh! he is an Indian." My grandfather himself was not a very big-sized man. He would look around and call out "Shyamlal"—that was one nephew— and "Maharaj"— that was the other. And these two hefty people would come and whoever was wanting this compartment just went away. Somehow these small things created a new atmosphere. It made people feel, "Although here is an empire which is so big, so powerful, yet we can stand up to it." And little by little the things were not small. They became bigger and bigger till the whole independence movement gained such a momentum that it was like the whole vast population of India moving, as the sea moves here, and there was absolutely no stopping it. And that is what finally brought us our freedom.

Now we need a movement like that to continue this fight for freedom. We are politically free but it is not complete freedom. We are still dependent for our economic advance. We have this drought and we have to get food from outside. To develop our industries we need so many things from outside. When we were involved in fighting on our border, although we have been making a large number of things ourselves, still we were dependent for many parts of essential equipment from abroad. And if people said, "You can't have it", we were stuck. So this is not my idea of freedom. My idea of freedom is a self-reliant nation. It is true no nation today can be fully self-sufficient. We shall have to have something from outside; but at least there should be a base of self-sufficiency and self-reliance. Here again there is something for our young people to do— to create an atmosphere of self-confidence. Each one of us by ourselves, each state by itself, does not have the strength or the resources. But when we are together as one whole, there is no power on earth which can stop us from going ahead. This is the choice in your hands. Do you face challenge courageously, or do you sit back and say "This is too big" and you get involved in lots of small problems? The language problem is very important to people; they are emotionally involved. It concerns their future, their jobs, their careers. Yet in the context of the whole of India and the problem of India's advance and India's liberty being strengthened, the language problem is a small problem.

I should like to speak about many more things to you but I think the time is now up. I would only say that when I took this tremendous job which I have now—which, as you have seen described in the newspapers, is really one of the toughest there can be in the world today—I did so without any fear, without any hesitation, because I thought that I would have the full support of the young people of India, because I thought that the young people had enough strength, enough courage, to see the country through these very difficult problems, that they had the will and would soon, with their education, have the knowledge to face these problems. If there were a short cut we could say, "This is an easier path, we can cut across, we needn't take the other long-winding path, so full of rigours." But there is no short cut. People who have tried to take short cuts in other countries have found them to be full of dangers and they found that in the long run a short cut is just as long, and really no shorter. We have taken the longer road: the road of democracy. We could have said when we became independent in 1947: "Here we are. We are popular. Nobody is questioning our right to do what we want." We could have had a dictatorship, or any form of government and perhaps it would have been easier to push through some programmes. But we deliberately made the choice of taking the longer and in some ways the more difficult path, which is the path of democracy, which gives the privilege and the right of choice to every single person, literate or illiterate, progressive or backward. No matter what language he speaks, no matter whether he is from the plains or from the hills, or is a tribal, to each person we gave the right of choice. We did so because we felt that in the long run this was what would strengthen the people, and would enable them not to put up with any kind of tyranny. It was not that we strayed into democracy or chose the path of planned development. These were well-thought-out, well-considered, well-argued decisions.

As we go ahead we shall find that each of these decisions has been a right decision. But the basic decisions which we took have been right and the proof is the large number of bright young people one sees around them.

I have posed many questions to you and it is for each one of you to find the answer which he or she thinks is the right answer. There may not always be the same answer. But whatever answer you find, from your own thinking, that will probably be the right answer for you. I should only hope that you will give these questions serious thought and that you will encourage amongst yourselves the habit of discussion. Amongst you there may be many who could find newer answers, better answers, more original answers. We need those answers. We do not say that our answers are the only right ones. Every few years new things are discovered, new methods are discovered. There is a tremendous responsibility on your shoulders. May you bear it lightly and may you bear it not only with courage but also with good humour.

3. CONVOCATION ADDRESS AT SANTINIKETAN*

My heart is filled with sorrow and foreboding at what is happening in Bengal today, which even the peaceful quiet of Amrakunja cannot remove. We are seized with passion. How can we ignore it? Yet at this auspicious moment and at this Amrakunja Samavartana (convocation), I do not think that politics is a fit subject for discussion and so have decided to speak on certain ideals. I am pained that even here politics has cast its black shadow.

Nothing in the world is entirely new and nothing in the world is changeless. This one sees in Santiniketan. It is certainly growing and changing, and yet, it retains a quality of gentleness, as if the beneficent spirit of Gurudev and Master Moshai† were even present. Gurudev was himself part of all time. He conversed with the sages of the dawn of our civilisation, yet he walked in the modern age. He combined the eternal and the immediate. He reconciled the universal with the local. That is why he gave the name Visva-Bharati to this great school. He wanted every

*Address as Acharya of Visva-Bharati at the convocation at Santiniketan, December 24, 1967.
†Guruder is Rabindranath Tagore, the poet. Master Moshai is Nandlal Bose, the painter.

student of this University to become a *visva-manava*, a universal individual who knew no narrowness and who could say: "The world is my home and all men are my brothers." But even the universal has to find identity of place and nationality, of shape and name. That is why the Poet was proud of being an Indian while aspiring to be a universal man. My father expressed the same idea in a different way when he declared that no one could be truly international unless he also was intensely national. This was true of Gurudev and of my father. For neither of them could think of realising the universe by escaping from his Indian identity. The Poet spoke once of finding freedom in a thousand bonds of delight. A thousand bonds of delight linked him to his motherland. Gurudev's creed was one of affirmation. His greatest dreams were dreamt for his country and for his fellowmen. In his poems and songs, in his letters and talks, he has described the India of his hopes and prayers. There can be no freedom without fearlessness, without knowledge and without the ability to seek and follow truth, though it might take one away from the old and the familiar. For to seek truth one must tear asunder the veils of prejudice and superstition.

Around us we find parochialism. In many parts of the country we feel the fever of chauvinism, be it linguistic or provincial, raging afresh at the smallest provocation. This spells danger. We must try to draw strength from the Poet who symbolised the greatest in contemplation and achievement. We must study anew his message and learn to rise above all meanness of spirit.

Through Visva-Bharati, Gurudev hoped to develop truly liberated individuals. That indeed should be the purpose of all universities. The liberated individual prizes freedom, that of others even more than his own. He chooses the path of reason and holds to morality with emotion, but eschews fanaticism. To him the equality of religions and races is second nature. Self-discipline and restraint are his true badge. In other words, he is a true democrat. Those who do not believe in the methods of peace and reconciliation cannot be true democrats. True democracy never allows the letter to pervert the spirit. As is said in the Corinthians, "Not of the letter but of the spirit: for the letter killeth, but the spirit giveth life."

I have drawn pointed attention to this because, as the years go by, there are fewer left among us who have received democratic education from the school of Gandhiji and Jawaharlal Nehru. Their teaching was that we could become a great nation and good individuals through the development of our inner resources. This development of inner resources, they believed, could come only through self-restraint. Gandhian Satyagraha is based on self-restraint. The essence of Satyagraha is controlled response to injustice. It is through control that the response becomes effective and eventually victorious. Self-restraint, again, is the essence of constitutional democracy as Jawaharlal Nehru envisioned it.

As we enter the third decade of freedom, certain over-simplified ideas of democracy have begun to gain currency. There is a feeling that whatever the people do is right. But the divine right of the people, which is enshrined in democracy, also requires that the will of the people be expressed through reflection and judgment. Every democratic system evolves its own conventions. It is not only the water but the banks which make the river.

If these conventions are flouted or disowned, democracy itself ceases to be. It is not democracy for the legislative chamber to be converted into the street; nor by any means can the street be the place where laws are made. The mob is thus a negation of democracy. Constitutions and conventions are intended to prevent violence and not to serve the cause of violence. My father said, "Democracy is the method of discussion, argument, persuasion and ultimate decision and the acceptance of that decision, even though it might go against our grain. Otherwise the bigger *lathi* or the bigger bomb prevails and that is not the democratic method. The problem is the same whether atomic bombs are involved or street demonstrations, but I object to their violence."

If democracy is to survive, we need a large body of mature individuals who are bound together by great objectives voluntarily accepted. Development, whether of a nation or an individual, consists in using one's resources and exerting oneself to the utmost. Within each one of us there is a stock of resources which is practically inexhaustible. Education, the combination of formal learning with the experience of life, is the process by which we learn to use these resources, not only for utilitarian, economic ends but for the attainment of those more intangible rewards which are aesthetic and spiritual. He who approaches education from the attitude of "What shall I get out of it?" gets very little. But he or she who approaches education with the attitude of "What shall I be able to give as a result of it?" will also get more. For it is through giving that we receive. In the words of Eliot:

In order to possess what you do not possess,
You must go by the way of dispossession.
In order to arrive at what you are not,
You must go through the way in which you are not.

After these years of preparation, you are entering the world of work, challenge and responsibility, a world of harsh contest and fleeting recompense. In life the chances of fulfilment and frustration are equal. If you follow the teachings of the illustrious founder of this institution, you will be able to transform even defeats into opportunities and ultimate victories. I wish you well.

In the realm of education, in religious and social reform, in cultural renaissance and political revolution, the great sons and daughters of Bengal have shaped our evolution. Along with millions of Indians, I too have been inspired by these saints and scholars, these sensitive, talented and rebellious spirits. Today, Bengal stands guard on our international frontiers. This places a heavy responsibility on her people to protect the security and integrity of our country. To the people of Bengal, from the high Himalayas down to the sea coast, my greetings and good wishes for the coming New Year. May it bring them peace and prosperity and opportunities for building a better life. Let us seek the blessings of Gurudev.

4. CONVOCATION ADDRESS AT ROORKEE UNIVERSITY

There was a time when I used to be puzzled by the practice of universities admitting persons from the rough and dusty world of politics to the community of academics. I even took it to be the mocking tribute of learning to power. Recently, I have begun to find an inner meaning in this gesture which saves it from being a mere ritual. This kind of ceremony is a symbol of the close relationship that should subsist between the university and the world of action. Those entrusted with the burden of practical affairs must take their problems to the universities. Universities in turn must teach men to see things in perspective. Implicit in the idea of a university is the habit of looking at least two or three generations ahead.

Roorkee is an institution with a name, a tradition and a distinctive record of service. Men have gone out from here and planted the seeds of change in many parts of the country, more particularly in the broad plains of the Ganges and the Indus. The canals they have dug, the roads they have laid out, the bridges they have built and the buildings they have constructed have made the earth fruitful, brought town and village nearer together and housed schools, factories and offices. In the beginning the men of Roorkee were apprentices to European engineers and technologists. Gradually they took over the work themselves and demonstrated their mettle and excellence. Their labour and devotion has kept pace with the expansion of public works in our northern region. More recently, as the process of development gained speed, Roorkee itself expanded from a college to a University with many departments under the inspiring guidance of people like Dr. A. N. Khosla and Shri G. Pande and the present Vice-Chancellor.

I should like to utilise this occasion to share some thoughts on the place of technology in our development. First, we might consider the contribution of technology to the task of transforming the economy. Secondly, the administrative environment in which engineers and scientists can best serve the community. Thirdly, the contribution of technology and science towards changing social attitudes and organisation. Fourthly, the relationship between the state of technology within our country and in the wider world.

In 1950 we earnestly took up economic planning. It was important for us to utilise science and technology to solve the problems of poverty and inequality. The first task of the Planning Commission, as listed in its terms of reference was to "make an assessment of the material, capital and human resources of the country, including technical personnel", and to investigate the possibilities of augmenting them. Our nationalist movement had for long realised that our ills could be cured only through the right use of science. Like many philosophers in the West, Mahatma Gandhi reacted against the first consequences of the Industrial Revolution. But even he saw the inevitability of technological advance. "What I object to is the craze for machinery, not machinery as such," he once declared. ". . . I want to save time and labour, not for a fraction of mankind but for all; I want the concentration of wealth not in the hands of the few, but in the hands of all . . . Scientific truths and discoveries should first of all cease to be mere instruments of greed." Our approach to economic planning was inspired by the great experiment in the Soviet Union. But never was there any doubt, whether at the time the National Planning Committee was set up by the Congress in 1937 or when the Government constituted the Planning Commission in 1950, that planning in India had to be Indian in its ethos, in its methods and its prescriptions.

The Industrial Revolution came to our country a century after it took root in Europe. The first railways, telegraphs and textile mills were established here in the middle of the last century. But the rate at which technology spread was very slow, compared with Japan where the Industrial Revolution had its beginnings about the same time. The reason was our political subjection. It is only after we became free and we began planning, that we gained speed. After the completion of the Third Plan, we are at a stage where the first Industrial Revolution is over and the second has begun. With some notable exceptions, we are today where the advanced nations were before the First World War. These exceptions are atomic energy and electronics, two fields in which we do not lag behind.

Great changes have occurred in our economy in the last twenty years. Production has expanded. Even more remarkable is the increasing diversity of the goods we produce. I shall not attempt to list the achievements of the years of freedom. But I should like to draw your attention to the change in social outlook which has accompanied economic change. A bullock-cart driver with a transistor radio is no longer an isolated sight. In the last few years the transistor radio has caught the imagination of our people. It is to be seen everywhere. The people want it not merely for the music and information it brings. To them it is a symbol of modernity and the world of plenty. It is a release from drabness and drudgery. Its vogue is proof of the fact that nowadays invention is the mother of necessity. We are reaching the stage where the first fruits of technology trigger a general demand for more technology.

It has been remarked that Britain and other European countries put through their Industrial Revolution without any considerable addition to the stock of science. Progress came mainly through the technological exploitation of known knowledge and its extensive application. Although we are on the threshold of the Second Industrial Revolution, which presupposes new findings in science, we have by no means exhausted the first task of extending known knowledge to all parts of the country and to all sections of the population. Irrigation, electrification, the making of primary tools for the farm and the factory and the building of low-cost houses; all this is the work of the technologist and the engineer rather than of the scientist. Indeed the bulk of the labour we have undertaken under the Five Year Plans falls on the shoulders of the engineer. So much so that planned development is often referred to as social engineering. This work is far from complete. We are proud that we have electrified 50,000 villages in the last fifteen years. This is no mean achievement, but it still leaves us with 500,000 more villages to electrify. The whole of the countryside of Madras is studded with electric pumps, but there are sixteen other States where this needs to be accomplished.

Recently, I invited forty eminent scientists and technologists from various fields of activity to discuss the problems of science and technology in India. Among the topics posed were the organisation and administration of science, the determination of priorities in research, the relationship of national laboratories and universities, the question of collaboration and patents, the methods of fostering the scientific temper and of combating superstition, ways of arresting the brain drain and the problem of the teaching medium of science.

This was too long an agenda for just a couple of days, nor do conferences of this kind probably come up with anything startlingly new. But when you bring together people of outstanding ability and knowledge, each keen on contributing the essence of his experience, there is a general gain in insight. It was a stimulating meeting. My main purpose was to find out how much truth there was in observations made to me that Indian science had come to a halt. I am convinced that we have people of the requisite calibre and force who can set things right. The meeting strengthened my belief that in all that the Government does it should use existing talent in the country more extensively and discourage the all too prevalent practice of looking to the outsider. Scientists on their part conceded that the laboratories had not yielded the results expected of them, but pointed out that the fault lay with the problem-setters rather than with the scientists.

Who are the problem-setters? We in Government, whether the politically elected representatives or the civil servants. Criticism of the inadequate scientific equipment on the part of the politician and administrator is not limited to our country. We hear it in Britain and Europe. We hear it in the United States. We hear it in the Soviet Union despite the increasingly larger place which engineers and scientists occupy in Government there. Sometimes the theories and ideologies on which

States are run hinder the fuller use of science. Sometimes it is the fault of systems and decision-making individuals. The civil servant is primarily the master of the short-term solution. The politician's horizon is sometimes not much larger. The vision of both is governed by what is practicable. The civil servant goes by precedent and notions of administrative feasibility. The politician is dominated by considerations of popular acceptance. Yet what is popular need not necessarily be right or wise. The immediate is often the enemy of the ultimate. Commonsense forms the basis of much of the judgment of civil servants and politicians. But commonsense is not necessarily scientifically valid. It becomes the duty of scientists and technologists to set the pace. They can do it through universities, through professional organisations which should make known their views on all subjects involving science and technology. They should do it through personal discussion. Some of the scientists who attended the round-table asked: "What will follow from these discussions?" In my view the usefulness of the meeting should be judged not merely in terms of certain decisions but in the impact it made on my own outlook and on the attitudes of the senior civil servants who were present. This benefit is substantial if less tangible. This helps in the education of those in public service.

The use of the expert is a major problem in public administration. I have no doubt that our present administrative system uses the expert inadequately and indifferently. It gives undue weight to the generalist and persists with criteria of competence developed in times when the range of government decisions was very limited and was unrelated to the demands of economic management and growth. Also, in the absence of responsible governments, the official class developed a mystique both of infallibility and of transferability of talent.

After we attained freedom, governmental responsibility suddenly expanded. The public sector was enlarged as a matter of deliberate choice. Officials were called upon to bear vast and new kinds of responsibility. Not many could be trained in the expert knowledge and scrutiny which their work required. Experts from outside were not assimilated fast enough into the service.

In spite of numerous attempts at reform, the administration still tends to be hierarchical and status-bound. Pay and power are equated, instead of pay and utility. It is odd that the greatest doctors and engineers in the country, who would be rated as the leaders of the profession and who save lives or add permanent assets to the nation, can rarely hope to receive the pay or status of Secretaries of Ministries. The brightest of our young men and women choose engineering and medicine. If they happen to go into Government, they are very soon overtaken by the general administrator. This must change and I am trying to change it. The administrative system must reflect an individual's contribution to human welfare and economic gain.

Having made the point, let me hasten to correct any apprehension that the technologist is ipso facto and in every way superior to the professional administrator or politician. The man trained to be a technologist may not necessarily be competent to decide on matters outside his specialisation. He may not be the best person to judge the social or political cost.

A great deal of administration consists in taking political decisions in the handling of men. The instincts and talents of leadership do not automatically flow from training in technology. Technology as such has no answers to political problems. Some scientists and technologists certainly possess qualities of social leadership of the highest order, but the abilities of most remain confined to their fields of specialisation.

I should like to see the technologist take very much more initiative in agricultural engineering. Our farmers are awake at last. They do not need to be preached to any longer. Most of them are converts to modern farming even before the evangelist approaches them. In fact the difficulty of the administration has been to meet this rising demand. In this situation the agricultural engineer can make great contributions to the wealth of the land and the well-being of individual farmers.

The industrial designer also has vast opportunity opening out before him. There are so many items which the people want. The industrial designer should devise ways of providing these goods at prices which the common people can afford.

Industrial designing is a comparatively new profession in our country. So far it has addressed itself only to the needs of the well-to-do sections. These sections are attuned to international norms of consumption, which are wasteful and inappropriate to our conditions. The imagination of the industrial designer can design a new range of articles for use in ordinary homes, schools and offices which not only save resources but narrow the gap between the affluent and the poor and thus make for a more egalitarian society.

It is the duty of every engineer and technologist to help the country to use resources economically. The wealth beneath the surface of the earth, the wealth of the forests, the wealth of the rivers, all this belongs more to posterity than to us. We have no right to squander it. Even in well-endowed America, the people are blaming the pioneers for the reckless way in which they exploited mineral and soil resources.

There has been a spectacular increase in the facilities for training in engineering and technology. In terms of numbers we might feel reasonably secure that our future development will not be stalled for want of qualified scientists and engineers, QSES as they are called in Britain. But we cannot be satisfied with the general quality of our trainees. This University and the prestigious I.I.Ts. are exceptions. In general, our engineering colleges, as indeed most of our educational institutions, are under-staffed, under-equipped and intellectually under-nourished. That even Roorkee cannot find enough teachers to fill the sanctioned strength highlights the gap between expectation and reward in the profession.

So far I have spoken of the role of technology in bringing about economic change, and of the conditions in which the scientists and technologists can give their best to the nation. The purpose of technology is to make and provide the goods and tools which a society needs. In so doing it goes beyond the merely utilitarian. In advanced countries, technology has increased the area of choice and satisfaction for people. It has begun to do so in our own country. If life is more open today than before it is not only because of our political system but also because of the economic progress we have already achieved. As the Scientific Policy Resolution so eloquently says, "Science has led to the growth and diffusion of culture to an extent never possible before. It has not only radically altered man's mental environment, but what is of still deeper significance, it has provided new tools of thought and has extended man's mental horizon. It has thus influenced even the basic values of life, and given to civilisation a new vitality and a new dynamism."

Jawaharlal Nehru, who inspired the Scientific Policy Resolution, saw science as a liberating force. The lines I have read out speak of enlarging mental horizons. Such an enlargement involves the shedding of old prejudices and fears. Science fights superstition. The unquestioning reverence of everything old is superstition. The notion that some races or religions or castes are superior to others is a superstition. The belief that a system of thought appropriate to one historical situation is of universal validity is a superstition. Science, on the other hand, is attuned to change.

For various reasons, superstition is entrenching itself and finding new supporters. Without the help of science, I see little hope of checking the virus of religious hatred. Scientists and technologists should make it their mission to spread the scientific temper so that our forward march is not blocked by obstacles of superstition.

Does all this mean unqualified praise of science? Some of you might ask: "But has not the machine swallowed meaning, and has not science brought the world to the brink of nuclear disaster?" Others might reflect on the growing technological disparity between the "have" countries and the "have not" countries and wonder whether the gap will ever be closed, and whether poverty can be conquered. These are legitimate questions. We believe in the commingling of the humanist and scientific traditions, of the best in the old and new. The more specialisation there is, the greater the need for a cross-fertilisation amongst different callings and disciplines.

The widening technological gap is a cause for anxiety. Whatever the relative distance between the levels of living in rich and poor countries, I believe the latter can and will banish hunger, illiteracy and ill-health. It is these which make poverty so unbearable, and not the absence of a plethora of material goods. The way of life in advanced countries is not always right. In fact we should resist and reject any such apotheosis of affluence. Nor should all nations attempt to create within their countries the type of life which exists in the advanced countries of today. We must summon the best findings of mankind's spiritual history to guard ourselves against the sense of futility and vacuum which seems to be pervading some countries. Everywhere the most sensitive minds feel concerned at the predicament of man in this nuclear age.

5.   ON A DOCTOR'S WORK*

When we speak of a doctor's work, we naturally wonder what kind of society he will serve. The doctor does not live in a vacuum. He is pre-eminently a servant of society, and he is in touch with humanity and human problems, which are often enough psychological problems. This is a physical truth. Men and women are constituted the same way all over

*This address was given at the All-India Institute of Medical Sciences, March 23, 1968.

the world, though there may be differences in the types of diseases, or the length of their life span. Most diseases around us are due to poverty and ignorance. People fall ill and die because of lack of knowledge, the callousness of society and our limited means.

When the gap between suffering and our ability to alleviate it is so immense, is it to be wondered that many in the medical profession feel frustrated? There is shortage of staff, of equipment, of drugs and of administrative support—it is a sad story. We need also to improve the working conditions of our doctors, not merely their pay, but the tools with which they function, reference libraries, the assignment of responsibility and a change in the set relationship between juniors and seniors, as well as between professionals and administrators—these are factors which give work-satisfaction.

I do not wish to underrate the achievements of our doctors and health administrators. As we all know, within a generation the average life span of our people has nearly doubled. Credit for this belongs to the medical community. You have largely taken the terror out of epidemics. The old belief that disease indicated the displeasure of the gods is on the way out. Today the common people crowd to doctors with faith and in the hope that you can work the miracles which priests and magic men could not. In fact, no other single group has so many demands made on it. There is no hospital or clinic which does not look like a beleaguered fortress!

The medical profession has made many positive gains in the last twenty years. We have set up new hospitals, opened an impressive chain of rural clinics, discovered the utility of well-planned national campaigns, such as the anti-malaria drive. No less notable is the expansion of our pharmaceutical industry and the surgical tools industry. But primarily, the change has been quantitative. We have not yet sought to make structural changes in the organisation of our medical services in relation to society. Our pattern of education and medical administration has remained roughly the same as it was under British rule, although in their own country the British themselves have made such changes. In India, we have been able to extend the idea of social responsibility for the individual's health to only very small sections of Government servants and some groups of industrial labour. For the rest, only those with means can buy health. There is much talk of speedy and inexpensive justice. This is important. But speedy and inexpensive medical care is an even greater priority.

Socialist countries have an excellent record in this matter. The medical services of the Soviet Union and the East European countries are most impressive, especially as regards the care taken of children and mothers. I am sure there are many innovations which we can adopt and adapt to counter-balance our dependence on Anglo-American methods, equipment and text-books. A beginning has been made in securing the co-operation of the Soviet Union in medical education, as also in the manufacture of drugs and surgical tools.

In medical education, our principal aim should be to produce a good foundation doctor who is equipped to meet basic health problems. A few of them will no doubt go on to be specialists in chosen fields. At the rate at which medical knowledge is advancing, no person can hope to be an all-rounder. But he should know the essentials, so as to make the work of specialists more full of purpose. The training of sound and self-reliant medical men, who regard the people as their responsibility, and do not seek to escape the rigours of their profession should be the first function of our medical colleges. We need to improve the general quality of medical graduates and to overhaul their training so as to enhance the value of their contribution to society.

Medical research is important but the interests of research and specialisation themselves require a strong base of general competence. We have an unfortunate tendency in our educational system to regard the secondary stage merely as a feeder to university education, and in university education to subordinate everything else to the production of Ph.Ds. Every high school imagines itself to be a potential post-graduate research centre, and is unfortunately neither one nor the other. There are complaints that the steep increase in medical college admissions has greatly outpaced the attention given to standards of teaching and training. Sometimes adequate importance is not given to practical training.

Let us not allow ourselves to be diverted from our basic task. The main medical problems of advanced countries are ailments of affluence and longevity, while ours are those of poverty and neglect. Each nation has to devise teaching and research patterns suited to its own needs. Our slender resources of money and men must be directed towards our own needs.

Modern medicine has advanced tremendously, almost, one might say, miraculously. It has grown on research, on experience. Research cannot afford to ignore any facts or data. Yet we in India do ignore to a large extent the storehouse of medical knowledge which we have inherited. We do not fully exploit the medicinal value of our plants or minerals. Our research should look into these matters, so that all that is of value can be preserved and modernised for the benefit of our people.

Besides raising teaching standards in medical colleges, we must strengthen the district hospital. A good hospital is like a great tree casting a giant shadow of protection, as the cathedral or the temple was in the Middle Ages. Are the district hospitals equipped to perform the three functions—emergency care, preventive service and curative work? We are naturally keen that medical care should reach the remotest villages in the plains and in the hills. But how can this be done effectively, unless there are well-run institutions at headquarters, adequately staffed and equipped with apparatus, drugs and reference literature? Doctors must be encouraged to go to villages. But they need a place to which they can turn. The district hospital can develop its mobile services so as to reinforce the work of the field doctor. Some of these points have, I believe, been gone into by the A.P. Jain Committee, whose report the Government is studying. On their part, doctors must also respond to the needs of the people, especially those in far-flung areas, even if it means inconvenience and discomfort. Life in villages can improve only if educated people go to live there and take interest in the overall improvement of the place.

Hospitals and medical colleges must play a greater role in preventive medicine. But medical students could render signal service by systematically undertaking the protection of the population from the more obvious of preventible diseases. Is there dichotomy in our administration between medical and public health services? An integrated view is essential, and there should be close relationship among teaching medical administration, public health services and research, which are all aimed at solving basic problems.

An example of a well-organised public health campaign is the anti-malaria programme. An anti-smallpox campaign has also been undertaken. There are other diseases such as tuberculosis, leprosy and filaria which require our urgent attention. I am told that owing to complacence at the third stage, malaria is coming back again. This is sad news and the Government and people need to bestir themselves. The battle for health is a continuous one, any slowing down will affect the whole nation.

Two other determining factors pertaining to the nation's health and well-being are family planning and nutrition. When talking about our country and its problems, let us remember that many of these problems are the result of our success and development. Our population problem is an example. As an eminent doctor has rightly remarked, doctors themselves are the creators of the population explosion. They must also find a way out. A child brings happiness. As Kabir the poet-saint has said, a child comes crying into the world but the people around are swathed in smiles. But such is the economic lot of the bulk of our people, that even the birth of a child adds to their anxiety. Our population figures cause knitted brows all over the world.

The aim of family planning is to restore joy to motherhood, and to make every child a wanted child, with a fair chance of health, education and employment. Until now our major difficulty was to create the motivation and psychological climate. Our campaign has been successful in certain pockets. It is not unlikely that soon a nationwide clamour for doctors and appliances for family planning will build up. Such a phenomenon has taken place in agriculture. Any delay or failure in the family planning campaign will cause a set-back to all our programmes.

Another important health problem is that of nutrition. Howsoever good one harvest may be, let us not forget that a large part of our people are chronically undernourished in terms of calories as well as life-building proteins. If nothing is done about this protein scarcity, these masses will remain condemned to an incomplete and lustreless life. I have pleaded for close co-operation between medical scientists and agricultural scientists in improving the nutritional value of our diet. In your own Institute, notable research work has been done in anaemia and nutritional deficiency. Work is also being done in the Nutrition Research Laboratory and elsewhere. Guided by the results of this research, we must evolve a programme to make up the vital nutritional deficiencies of school-children and mothers.

Why have you chosen medicine as a career? Surely not merely out of expectation of gain or of fame. These come to the successful in any profession. What must have influenced your own decision is a special sympathy with other people and an urge to alleviate their suffering. Guard and cherish that gift of sympathy. For it is given to doctors, more than to all others, to appear in the people's prayers. I wish each one of you the doctor's true reward—a life not of ease but of work and the great satisfaction that because of your effort, many have found life and health. One gets from it what one gives to it. I hope therefore that you will regard your work not just as a profession but will give to it your utmost in endeavour and interest.

6. FAMILY PLANNING*

It is a pleasure to be amongst persons who are dedicated missionaries of our country's future. Mrs. Dhanvanthi Rama Rau and her colleagues do not need to be preached to or exhorted on the virtues of family planning. Their own pioneering work has largely been responsible for the Government and the people of India recognising the vital connection between family planning and planning for the country's prosperity. In fact, Shrimati Rama Rau is the founder of the International Planned Parenthood Federation.

This conference serves the very useful purpose of bringing together workers, non-official leaders, administrators and policy-makers in this field to take stock of the progress, to analyse the problems and to search for solutions.

Family planning is an accepted official policy in India. But our programme will not succeed if it remains only an official programme. There are some development plans which can be taken up and completed by a few for the many by the Government. But family planning is truly a people's programme. Its success rests on individual citizens. They have to be approached, persuaded, prompted and helped to practise family planning. The entire official machinery for family planning, whether at the Centre or in the States, is meant for this task of persuasion and assistance.

In agriculture we have recently seen that the people's willingness to adopt new methods has overtaken official efforts. This might possibly happen in the family planning programme also.

Our farmers were not moved by the consideration of making the country self-sufficient in foodgrains. They took to new methods when they were convinced by the evidence of their own eyes that these larger harvests meant more profit for them. Similarly with regard to family planning, our people will not be greatly impressed merely by learning that a rate of

*This speech was given at the Sixth All-India Conference on Family Planning at Chandigarh, November 30, 1968.

growth of population of the order of a million a month poses problems for the nation. It should be proved to every village and every family that a smaller, more compact family makes for better health and greater happiness for the family hence more prosperity for the village.

In fact the very significance of calling our movement *family planning* and not population control is that our aim is to secure the welfare of our people. And since the family is the most real and enduring of human institutions we naturally have to achieve this welfare in terms of the happiness of children, wives and husbands. You will find the women of our country to be very responsive to any programme of action which ensures the health and future of their children.

We have achieved impressive success in terms of numbers since we took up the family planning programme three or four years ago with the urgency and earnestness it deserves. But the success has been limited as far as I can see to certain pockets. The most affluent sections of our population and perhaps those groups which are driven by the desire to improve their standard of living, namely the urban middle class and the skilled industrial workers are the ones most forthcoming to take advantage of the facilities offered by the Government.

Whoever wants to practise family planning should certainly be enabled to get proper advice and assistance. But the problem is not solved if we restrict our attention to such people. We must reach those groups who are in the most need of family planning, rather than those people who are the easiest to reach.

Any new scheme or project, any programme which promises improvement in the living levels of the people is taken advantage of by those who are already slightly better off. Higher education helps the urban middle class more than the rural working class. The practices of intensive agricultural production are utilised by those who already have the advantage of irrigation rather than by the farmers who are dependent on rain. Even such a good thing as a library helps only the literate and leaves the illiterate untouched. Thus many of our development plans often leave the poorest and weakest where they are, while the slightly better off become stronger. In the process, disparities increase. That is why the official and voluntary agencies—the latter even more—must strengthen their effort to reach those who are in the greatest need. Official agencies will be in a hurry to fulfil their targets. Non-official agencies may be better able to appreciate the human side of the problem.

The theme of your conference is "Family Planning for 100 Million Couples". We cannot proceed without targets. But the danger of targetry is that in the quest for figures, the desirable is subordinated to the practicable. It is true that you can show better results in the areas around Bombay, Delhi and Calcutta and other cities. But intensive work is even more necessary in very backward and highly populated areas, such as the eastern districts of U.P. A second danger of the target approach is that too little attention is given to the stabilisation of gains through follow-up and maintenance checks.

We should not be unduly influenced by the forecasts, mostly pessimistic, often made about our problems and shortcomings by superficial observers. We must proceed with our work according to our best judgment. In the advanced nations family planning and economic development were practically unrelated. Therefore they could offer us very little guidance. There, Society, Church and State were all opposed to family planning, and yet the birth rates fell because married couples wanted smaller families. This is true of Protestant-Puritan countries, Catholic countries as well as Socialist countries, all of which frowned on family planning. Yet family planning was practised in all these countries. The compelling reason was that progress already made prompted them to ask for more progress. Our own country, so marked by mass poverty, cannot leave it to individual motivation—because such motivation comes only after a certain level of literacy or economic betterment has already been reached. Japan achieved its spectacular advance in the last two decades because of universal literacy and its rise in the development ladder.

It is because we cannot afford to wait until such consciousness becomes widespread, that we in India require well-planned official programmes, which are implemented with determination. We have several advantages. Unlike the countries of the West, there is no organised religious opposition. Also, the educated person, especially the doctor, enjoys high prestige and his or her judgment carries weight.

The biggest enemy of family planning is the lassitude of our people. Even when they are convinced of the benefits of a course of action they make little attempts to exert themselves. Their enthusiasms are often short-lived. The high lapse ratio is a serious problem. This is the reason for our search for a device that has long-lasting effect.

A new danger to the family planning movement has been discernible for some time and it shows the link which politics has with all other aspects of life. There is propaganda to the effect that the family planning programme will upset the relative population ratios of the various groups in our country and thus weaken the political power or bargaining position of these groups. This pernicious doctrine may well convince people because of its very fallacy. History shows ample proof of the spread and influence of false beliefs. Workers in the field and all those interested in the family planning programme must strive to the utmost to combat this sort of propaganda and allay these imaginary fears.

The control of one's family gives greater opportunities for education and medical care and is equally important for all groups whether minority or not.

Simultaneous progress in programmes of intensive agriculture and family planning can give us the chance of conquering rural poverty. The one cannot be thought of as a substitute for the other.

In the agricultural programme, the combined efforts of extension agencies and of scientists produced good results. In the family planning programme also, the field programmes must be strengthened—the training of workers, the setting up of more teams, the production and distribution of family planning appliances, the use of the mass media to impart information and to create the right social climate. Equally important is biological research. For the last hundred years or so, medical research has concentrated its energies on combating death and alleviating pain. In the last few decades, science has also turned its attention to improving agricultural production. Science must now concentrate on the mysteries of birth so that individual families can regulate their size, nations can regulate their populations, and this planet itself determine how many people it should support and at what levels of happiness. Grotesque pictures are being painted of a world in which by AD 2000 which is not too far away from now the bulk of the people will be dying of starvation. The latest is Sir C. P. Snow's speech at the University of Missouri. This is a great challenge to science not only in our own country but all over the world.

Our success depends upon close co-operation between official and voluntary organisations.

7. CAN INDIA SURVIVE?*

It is a little difficult to know what to say about India in a few minutes.

*Informal talk at the Indo-French Colloquium organised by the Indian Council for Cultural Relations and the India International Centre in New Delhi, December 13, 1969.

I think all of you are aware that it is a country of many complexities and contradictions. No matter what one says it can be true of one part of India or another and yet be untrue for India as a whole. And one of the reasons, perhaps, why there is not better understanding of what we are doing or attempting to do is that most people who come to India and even the reporting that is done on India notice some scene or incident isolated from the historical perspective or from the larger image of India. We are today, perhaps, better placed in many ways than we have been for several years. The economic situation is more buoyant than it has been for some time. Our agricultural harvest has been remarkable and in almost every direction there are visible signs of progress. Yet, whenever anybody reports, especially the foreign newspapers, on India, the one headline that predominates is: Can India survive? Will democracy survive in India? One American columnist said a short while ago that of all the countries in the world it was only India about which this question was being constantly asked. It was only India which had to prove itself somehow time and again and even though we undertook something that was unexpected or that was considered too big for us, and even if we succeeded in it, the question arose with regard to the next step.

I inherited many good things from my father. One of them, let me tell you is love for France, French language and other things. But I think the most precious gift was tremendous confidence in the people of India. And I have no doubt that this country, which has faced great storms in its long history will always be able to weather whatever new storms burst upon us. Just now, to some people the political situation seems to be insecure or difficult to understand. Actually I do not think it is so at all. What has happened recently was in the making for many years. In fact, it began immediately after Independence. As in all countries, there were different points of view. Only in India the Congress Party was like an umbrella which had covered under itself many different points of view. That is one common factor of winning political independence. Even before Independence, there were different ways of functioning and thinking and there were different groups. But after Independence, this became very much—I mean the vision became very much sharper.

If I can take you into personal confidence, I will tell you a personal anecdote. There was much talk that because my father did not perhaps agree with every sentiment of Mahatma Gandhi, Mahatma Gandhi did not wish him to be the Prime Minister. I heard this gossip and I went to

Mahatma Gandhi and said: "If you do not want him to be the Prime Minister, you should say so openly and I think he should resign immediately, because at this moment only someone you want should be the Prime Minister." Mahatma Gandhi's reply was immediate and very clear. He said: "I have made my own opinion very clear. I have said that I do not think anybody else can be Prime Minister at this moment. But even if I did not think so, I have neither the authority nor the power to make a change—because this choice is the people's choice and although people will listen to much that I say, I doubt very much if they will listen to me if I go against your father." Then he said this sort of thing will always happen and I should not be concerned about it. So this kind of thinking along two lines was present from the very beginning. The question is: Did my father take the party or the country in a direction which Mahatma Gandhi did not want? On all basic issues, they agreed entirely: on the issue of removal of poverty and particularly how to do it, on the issue of what we call secularism and that we could never be aligned with any party which believed in one religion or one race or one language. This was the very basis of secularism, democracy and socialism—though socialism is understood in slightly different meaning. Where the difference did come in was that Mahatma Gandhi believed in a sort of decentralisation—improvement of village life without heavy industry. But I personally think that he said these things more because he had not gone deeply into the matter. Anyone who looks at Indian conditions knows that there was no means of giving a better life to the villagers unless we had industry, unless we produced within the country the things which our farmers and our other groups in the country needed to improve their living standards. The only other way was to buy those things from outside which meant foreign exchange, which we did not have, and which meant dependence on other nations, which we did not want to have. So the road that we took was, I think, the only possible road in the circumstances of India. In these years, much has been achieved and much has to be achieved. Where we have failed is not that we went in for industry or anything like that, but that we were not able and in fact we did not really even attempt to do a very important thing, which is to educate the people in a broader sense. For instance, we have various attitudes of mind which are anti-social, which are barbaric even, I would say, and Mahatma Gandhi had fought against them all his life. For instance, the attitude towards untouchables whom he called the Harijans. We put a clause in our Constitution that untouchability was illegal. At least I can speak for myself, that we and my family and hundreds of other families had changed their attitude and have never thought about it since. But the effort was not made to educate people in a deep and meaningful way about these matters with the result that although today every Government has to have at least one Minister from this class, there are certain number of reservations in offices and education, and other training programmes have expanded very much for these people, even so the attitude of mind about them does remain in many areas and even in some cities. This has been, I think, one of our major failures. There is nothing that can be done about this now except to take up this sort of education. It would not be true to say that even this class has not changed because they have changed.

The greatest change that has come about is not the big buildings or the industry or the production or the increase in exports or the agricultural revolution but the greatest change is in the minds of the people and no-body can have a conception of that unless they have lived in villages or in orthodox families before Independence. I went as a girl and sat on a bed in a Harijan household. They would wash that bed although I came from a higher caste, because the thought was implanted in their mind that any mixing of the classes is bad whether it is a higher class or a lower one.

So when you have had that kind of attitude and now you have the attitude that we have a right to equality, we have a right to the implanted privileges of citizenship and so on, that is one of the biggest changes. It is also of course one of the greatest difficulties facing the Government because whereas in France, and perhaps in other countries, you were able to have a certain amount of industry before the people's demands came to the forefront, we started with political consciousness of a very high order, not limited to a few people but which permeated right down to village, hills and everywhere because our Independence struggle, as you know, was not confined to a small group but it really was a mass struggle, in every meaning of the word "mass".

So we are confronted today with this very acute awareness among the people. We hear the phrase sometimes that the rich have become richer and the poor poorer. This, I am afraid, is not a fact. But what is the fact? The fact is that rich have grown richer, many people who were not so rich have grown richer. Many people who were, I won't say poor but certainly the middle class, have also got richer. Even amongst the poor many people are in a much better situation but those who lack things are more acutely aware of the lack than they were before. It was not that they did not lack them. Maybe, they had much less before but at that time they thought it was God's will and now they are aware that it is something that can be done and they are extremely angry that it has not been done. Of course, there was no way possible to do it in twenty-two years even if we had had a bloody revolution or any kind of "ism" or any kind of path. There was simply no way to do it in fewer years and even now there is no short-cut to it. We are fully aware whatever steps we take are merely tools which we think will bring us nearer to this goal.

Now the Indian character is such that people see things in extremes. If something is good then they will praise it to the skies; if it is not good, then they think nothing can be worse. And so if you take any steps, as for example when we nationalised fourteen banks, there is excessive popular expectation. Nobody in the Government, and certainly not myself, believed that that is going to create a revolution in India. It is a step which we thought was necessary. It was necessary because we were not able to effectively work out the previous steps taken. Had we been able to work social control as originally envisaged, we would not have had to nationalise the banks but because that was not done as it should have been, this became a political as well as an economic issue and it became inevitable. But immediately the sort of response that came about in the country was unexpected and a little bit alarming even, because although through these banks we do now have some funds which can go to give credit to sectors of population which did not get credit before —the smaller farmer and the poorer sections in the cities—obviously we can touch only a very very small fringe of the population. We cannot say that the difficulties of the poor will go or that poverty will be wiped out, but this is the type of reaction which is visible in the people.

Today one of the greatest obstacles is the cynicism of our intelligentsia, because no matter what is done they always look at it as something that is of no account. And this opinion is reflected in our press and it does have an influence on the people. In fact, one of the strange things that has happened is that our press is so entirely divorced from the people. It does not express what the people as a whole think. But this has happened to most, in fact all, our political parties. I do not think that there is any single paper which I would say has really kept itself in touch with the people's thinking and on the whole I think it is a bad thing. They should be in touch with what the people are thinking. But what is a good thing is that the people have not remained where they were. They have gone ahead regardless of the political parties. There is a momentum in the country which nobody can stop—none of the politicians or intellectuals or anybody else.

What I have done in my own party was not to split it; on the contrary, I tried desperately hard for three years to prevent this split which I could see coming. In fact it nearly happened even in my father's time. But I thought that it would be a bad thing for the country, and I tried to prevent it until a situation arose where the party was really getting so far from the people, that I could not see the Congress Party surviving even till 1972, till the next elections. And that is why I had to insist on something and even then it is not I who asked the people who are with me to split the party but the others who decided to go and sit with the Opposition. If I may say so, I think they showed rather unseemly haste in doing so. Had they continued for about a week till they got their proper seats, I do not think that anybody would have misjudged their intentions or judged it to be a weakness on their part and the things like that. But on the very first day in the Parliament they made a great dramatic show by sitting with the Opposition and it is not without point that the Opposition they sat with is the extreme rightist Opposition—the two parties which are in different ways entirely opposed to anything which Mahatma Gandhi stood for. I am specially mentioning this because Mr. Minoo Masani here raised the cry "back to Gandhi". So it is worthwhile knowing what Gandhiji stood for. He may not have stood for socialism as we understand it in the sense of the State having some of the means of production, but he did believe that nobody should have property. In fact he went some steps further when he said quite clearly that he thought that people should have these things as a trust. But if it did not work out, then buildings and other things could be taken away and he saw no reason why any compensation should be given at all. He said after all they made this money from the people and things belong to the people and there is no question of compensation. These are his words and not my words. But Government does give compensation and rather heavy compensation, if I can put it that way.

Well the Swatantra does not matter really because it is a party which has no future. It was in a way still-born from the beginning. But the party which is dangerous is the right-wing Jana Sangh, and it is dangerous because it appeals to the religious emotions of the people. And when a person thinks of religion in an emotional way, he is swept off his feet.

He cannot think logically or rationally and this is the great danger of the Jana Sangh.

We may be able to change their thinking. I do not know. They have changed quite a lot in recent years. They started off being very conservative in their economic policy but lately they have been saying that they believe in socialism. Only they do not think that we are socialists and we do not follow it properly. First, they were against the very concept of planning. Now they say: No, planning is good; but our plans are bad. In foreign policy also they were against our policy of non-alignment and they were for a pro-western attitude. Over the last year they have been saying that they believe in non-alignment but we are not certainly non-aligned. So in any way it is several steps forward and in most of my public speeches when I criticised them I have said I am not against the Jana Sangh, as indeed I am not against any party as such. I am against certain ideas which I consider to be bad for national unity or national strength. That is why as long as the Jana Sangh talks about the superiority of one religion or the people of one religion, about the majority community being first-class citizens and the others being second-class citizens, on that point I am certainly going to oppose them with all my strength and I hope I am not immodest when I say that it was largely due to my efforts in the last mid-term polls that we were able to reduce Jana Sangh's seats both in Bihar and U.P., for which they cannot forgive me. And there is no occasion when they have come to me on other matters, when they have not said: "Why do you hit us?" And I tell them that it is only for these reasons, and if you change, well, you have a right to think like us on economic matters or any important matter. It is a democratic country but just religious opposition is very bad for us, as we have seen in the last communal riots that we had. It is something which eats away the very foundations of our nation.

While we are settling down, the people are maturing politically; the people are being strengthened. The example I gave of the Jana Sangh is a telling instance. They changed certainly not because of my speeches. They could not care less what I said. They changed because they felt that the people would not allow them to hold certain ideas. They started off by being against bank nationalisation. But they found that they could not go back to their constituencies; they could not say they were opposed to this measure. This is how the people themselves are bringing about these changes.

Obviously, the people are not at one level. Many of our Swatantra Party M.P.s are elected from areas in Bihar which they had never visited before. They do not even speak the language of the people. They know nothing about it. But they were elected from those areas because people are economically backward and less politically conscious than in other parts. There are within any country different levels of development. Again, if I may give an example, in 1950 I went to a place in N.E.F.A. where the very first wheel that the people saw was the wheel of our Dakota plane. They had no conception of anything round, although they had a fairly developed irrigation system of their own. But they had never worked a wheel. They had not seen a cart or anything like that. That was in 1950. But today they have got jeeps. You cannot say that those people are as politically conscious as people in Delhi or Bombay, or in Bihar or U.P. So when you think of India, you must have this in the background. You cannot think of India without keeping all this bewildering diversity in mind.

Now, obviously, I cannot prophesy about India's future except to say that I have great confidence in the people. And I have no doubt that whatever happens, they will come out on top. And that is what matters. One of the points of disagreement between me and some of our party bosses was that right in the beginning, soon after becoming Prime Minister, I made a speech in Bombay. I said that the Congress is very dear to me because some people joined it at the age of fifteen, some people at the age of twenty and some at forty or fifty. But I was born in the Congress. There was no time when my home, since I was born, was not the centre of all the major political movements, decisions and the meetings that took place and the whole of modern Indian history was being made there. People from all over India—peasants and others—were constantly coming. I was meeting them. I was in touch with their problems and so on. Nobody could be closer to the Congress or even more emotionally involved than I have been and I still am. But even so, I do feel that the country is more important than the Congress. If the Congress serves the needs of the country, it is right, we are with it. But if it does not, we cannot say that this is more important than India or the people of India. And many people resented this remark of mine and felt that it was disloyalty to the party. But still I feel strongly on this matter and I think the reason why the Congress went away from the people was partly because of being in power for a long time perhaps, but also because our type of democracy gives an easy foothold to what in America is called 'bossism'—that is everywhere a few people identify themselves with the party to the exclusion of all others, and claim that they alone can speak for the people of the state—rightly or wrongly, that is not for others to judge. We started losing in State after State and I saw no way in which we would bridge that gap except by going once more direct to the people. If I had the time I would have gone into why we lost in Bengal, for instance. Everybody knows why we lost in a State like Kerala. Perhaps you have not heard what happened in Pondicherry. Perhaps you being French, you may be a little interested in Pondicherry. It is a very small place. It is a charming French provincial town. We had a Congress Chief Minister there. He was a young Congress Muslim. For no reason, suddenly some of our people decided that he must go. "He is not the right person and it was a mistake for him to become the Chief Minister." Now I said: "Well. He is there. He has got elected. Now you wait for the next elections and you put up somebody else at the next elections." But they said: "No, no. He must go," and I was unable to help him and I tried very hard with the party. But the then leader made up his mind, with the result that the Government fell because the other person was not acceptable. There was re-election. Now we have the same young man as the Chief Minister but he is not in the Congress but he is in the D.M.K. He has Ministers and his Ministers who were in the Congress are now D.M.K. So his set-up practically is the same but instead of a Congress Government it is the D.M.K. I am giving this example to point out that the boss mentality went against the people's wishes and created a situation where you got less and less in touch with the people.

I have taken a great deal of your time. I want to congratulate the organisers of this Colloquium on this excellent idea and I hope that Indian transcendentalism and French logic working together might perhaps give a better perspective to our contemporary world.

8. CONVOCATION ADDRESS AT THE KASHI VIDYAPITH

The Kashi Vidyapith enjoys a special position among our educational centres. It has intimate connections with the freedom movement. Its graduates have served the nation with a devotion all their own and carved out a place for themselves in the people's hearts. I cannot but pay my homage on this occasion to Shri Lal Bahadur Shastri. Just two days ago we observed the fourth anniversary of his death. He symbolised the values which Dr. Bhagwan Das and the other founders of the Vidyapith had in mind when they established it.

This is one of the world's oldest cities. It is a city which makes us think of what is history and what is civilisation. Kashi stands on the river of India, the Ganga. It is regarded as the holiest of the holy cities of the Hindus. But even during Ashoka's time, it had already become a sacred place for the Buddhists.

So the mention of Varanasi brings to mind not only a picture of the Ghats along the Ganga but that of the serene Buddha figure of Sarnath. It brings to mind not only a vision of the dynamic monk Shankaracharya but of Kabir. He was a weaver by profession, in this home of brocades, and he taught us that the fabric of India has strands of more than one religion and that Ram and Rahim are woven into the prayers of our people.

Varanasi also brings to my mind the fact that the first college of modern education was founded here. I am reminded of Raja Rammohun Roy. He came here to study our ancient scriptures in their purity, but he became convinced that this nation could not live by its traditional knowledge alone. It is this realisation which made him the First of the Moderns.

As I contemplate the history of Varanasi three other faces come before me—those of Mrs. Annie Besant, Pandit Madan Mohan Malaviya and Mahatma Gandhi. Annie Besant was in a way complementary to Rammohun Roy. She proclaimed that man cannot live by modern knowledge alone, but needed the wisdom that had been discovered and bequeathed by the ancient sages and seers. Malaviyaji tried to blend the two in his university.

By a remarkable historical coincidence the very first gathering of the leading lights of Malaviyaji's university heard some plain speaking from Mahatma Gandhi. He had just come back from South Africa. His spectacular achievements there had been hailed, but few realised then that he was to play the same role on the much vaster stage of India. He was still an unknown quantity in India. And so when he spoke of our social responsibility and especially our duty not to flaunt wealth, it caused much resentment. Annie Besant and Malaviyaji themselves were very uncomfortable.

But within a year or two the country was to find itself dominated by this intruder who challenged us to look around and identify ourselves with the poorest and the most oppressed, who told us that if only the people of India listened to the still small voice within them, they could defy the might of empire.

It is out of this heightened awareness of our social responsibility and out of this sense of challenge that this centre of learning was born nearly fifty years ago. Its aim was to mould and fashion a new type of Indian. It is appropriate that we should take stock of the social scene of our day and also examine to what extent we have succeeded in moulding the new kind of Indian.

I had occasion recently to tell a gathering of scientists that there need be no conflict between the Indian man and the modern man, nor indeed the universal man. On the banks of the Ganga thousands of years ago our sages proclaimed that the world is one family. They taught us that change is the law of life. They evolved the symbol of the ever-turning wheel to tell us of the meaning of Dharma. In our own days a philosopher who lived and worked in this city, Dr. Radhakrishnan, advised and admonished us not to be prisoners of the past but pilgrims of the future. Yet at this same place a few days ago we heard propounded a new theory of the Indian, a theory which denies Indianness to hundreds of thousands of children of India. This doctrine of discrimination and hatred has to be fought with all our might. It is this kind of discrimination which had weakened our society in the past and sapped it of creative strength. Are we to suppose that Hindus alone are Indians and Muslims and Christians are not?

Who then is an Indian? Under the law everyone born in our land and every child of Indian parents is an Indian, irrespective of religion, race or sex. This concept of everybody's absolute equality in law is a magnificent concept, one of which we should be proud. It is only if we work ceaselessly to make sure that members of every minority and tribe feel absolutely sure and confident that they are accepted without question as full members of the Indian family that we can claim to be a "dharmabhoomi" and the world's largest democracy. "Dharma" is a comprehensive word. It does not mean religion alone but comprises law, duty, compassion, service and spiritual enlightenment.

My view of Indianness is not confined to the legal interpretation of being born within a geographical area or the constitutional imperative of accepting the equality of all citizens. To me Indianness implies a positive duty to understand and honour other points of view in consonance with the injunction that the ways to Truth are many. As our ancient books proclaimed, *Ekam sat, viprah bahudha vadanti.* Kabir and Nanak pointed out this same truth five hundred years ago. Vivekananda and Mahatma Gandhi have shown it to us in our own times.

Thus freedom from fanaticism and a capacity for acceptance and assimilation have been the genius of the Indian people. The Indian race itself is the complex product of many races. So is Indian culture a composite product of many forces and influences. One has only to hear our music and poetry and see our vast treasures of art and architecture to realise it.

It is this same capacity which, I am sure, will enable us to absorb the teachings of modern science without giving up our own moorings and our identity. They say art is local while science is universal. As technology develops and people all over the world use the same kinds of products of technology, offices and factories, airports and homes tend to look alike. The fashionable young of all countries appear to wear the same kind of clothes and grow the same kind of beards. The sociologist Herbert Marcuse tells us that modern technological culture is nonentitising us. Yet, if we only look closely, we see a desperate struggle for identity on the part of people, a struggle to retain their individual self against the pressures of the big machine and the all-powerful over-organised State, and also their own regional and local identity. In such a small country as Britain, the Scots will insist on wearing tartans, the Welsh will not give up their language. And in our own country, there is a special colour combination in the saris of Kanchipuram, a special flavour of cooking in the food of Punjab, a special rhythm of its own in the dance of Manipur, a distinctive style in the music of Banaras. People will not give them up. Nor need they give them up.

A Western thinker has defined philosphy as the process of describing the Universe. Philosphy and science, in the process of describing the Universe and finding out the truth, help us to understand which is essential and which is peripheral.

It seems to me that much of the thought expounded by the Vedas and the Upanishads is as relevant and contemporary today as the findings of the great modern scientific thinkers. The message of Gautama Buddha was not meant to be restricted to the Magadha of his day. Spiritual truth and scientific truth merge and had to merge. Thought that will not permit the growth and dissemination of knowledge cannot be the basis of knowledge. The aim of man should be constantly to seek eternal knowledge as well as new understanding. It is only through rational endeavour that life can find fulfilment and be redeemed from its ordinariness.

To the Hindus the Ganga is a symbol not only of truth eternal but also of the culture of our land. As Jawaharlal Nehru said in his will:

> The Ganga specially, is the river of India, beloved of her people, round which are intertwined her racial memories and her hopes and fears, her sense of triumph and her victory and defeat. She has been a symbol of India's age-long culture and philosophy, ever-changing, ever-flowing and yet ever the same Ganga.

Jawaharlal Nehru was proud of his Indian heritage, but he wanted to be heir not only to the best in India but to the best of all countries of the world.

Much of the confusion in our social and political life is due to the fact that we do not go deep into questions but seek refuge in ready-made solutions, our own as well as foreign. Instead of making a searching analysis of social, political and economic problems, we tend to interpret them in terms of personalities. We live in a complex political situation. It is natural that the changes, development and progress that have occurred over the last 22 years should raise new problems. We need a new outlook and new methods to deal with them. The response of some has been dynamic and radical but others are unable to get out of the rut. And so there is conflict. This conflict between the forces of change and the forces of *status quo* is not confined to India but is found in all countries of the world. Our country is as alluring as it is vast—and the times we live in are filled with marvels as well as excitement. Each day brings events which are a challenge to our imagination, courage and devotion to the country.

My appeal to you as graduates, teachers and students of Kashi Vidyapith is that you should propagate the concept of universal man, which is wholly compatible with the concept of an Indian as taught by Gandhiji, Dr. Bhagwan Das, Jawaharlal Nehru and Narendra Deva. I hope that the wisdom you have gained in this Vidyapith will help you to face the world's difficult and complex problems. You must have the courage to fight for your beliefs and to test your theories against the touchstone of reality. If the reality does not fit into your own frame of thought, it is not reality that can be given up but your way of thinking that needs to be changed. So long as we do not accept the reality we cannot succeed in solving the country's many problems. There is no problem that does not have a solution. You have to hope, you have to dare and you have to have faith in the country.

CHAPTER FIVE

The Congress Party

1. INTRODUCTION

DURING THE FIRST THREE YEARS OF MRS. GANDHI'S PRIME
ministership, there were differences of policy and temperament between
her and the Old Guard of the Congress Party. The party managers expected the prime minister to be guided by them. They were far to the right of
Mrs. Gandhi, who had inherited Jawaharlal Nehru's socialist objective.

The need to elect a new president of the Republic after the unexpected
death of Dr. Zakir Husain in May 1969 became an occasion for a direct
confrontation between the Old Guard and the prime minister. The
All-India Congress Committee, the national council of the Congress
party, met in Bangalore in July in a tense atmosphere. Mrs. Gandhi sub-
mitted a note on economic policy for discussion at the session, and the
note contained an outline of the radical measures which she was soon to
initiate. The speech which is published here explains the scope of the note.

The party chairman, Mr. S. Nijalingappa, had originally announced
that no decision would be taken in Bangalore on the Congress candidate
for the presidential election. But he decided to rush matters. Against the
wishes of Mrs. Gandhi, the Congress parliamentary board decided in
favour of the candidature of Mr. N. Sanjiva Reddy, speaker of the House
of the People (Lok Sabha), by a narrow majority. After returning to
Delhi from Bangalore, Mrs. Gandhi dropped Mr. Morarji Desai, the
finance minister, from the Cabinet and nationalised fourteen major banks.
As the clash of wills gained in intensity, Mrs. Gandhi suggested that
Congressmen who participated in the election of the President be given
freedom to vote according to their conscience. The prime minister's
supporters voted largely for Mr. V. V. Giri, and Mr. Sanjiva Reddy was
defeated. Thereupon, the party chairman expelled two ministers, who
were also members of the party executive, for defiance of the party

97

mandate. Mrs. Gandhi and her supporters demanded the convening of the All-India Congress Committee to discuss these developments. Mr. Nijalingappa refused to do so, and in early November he expelled Mrs. Gandhi herself. The letter which is published in this volume is one which Mrs. Gandhi addressed to her party colleagues setting out her point of view.

Nearly three-fourths of the members of the All-India Congress Committee supported the demand for a meeting. When this was rejected by Mr. Nijalingappa, they held a separate meeting. Thus two separate organisations, the Ruling Congress and the Organisation Congress, were born.

2. THE ROLE OF THE CONGRESS PARTY*

We all know what efforts the Congress has been trying to make and what things have been achieved. But what is the impression in the mind of the public? Are we concerned with it as a political body or is it something which we can afford to ignore? This is the question before us. We have talked very glibly about socialism for a long time. But, whatever our beliefs, and I certainly do not want to question anybody's bona fides or sincerity, does the public think that we are a socialist body? Does the public think that we are going in the socialist direction? This is the question.

The Congress is indeed a unique organisation. What has made it unique? Not merely its programme, not merely its leadership, although we have had the good fortune and the privilege of having some of the greatest men of the world as our leaders. But what marked out the Congress was that from the beginning it identified itself with the real basic problems of our people. We have not moved away from that aim. It is still our aim. The President rightly said that we are all concerned about the down-trodden. Yet, when we look at where we have come—and I do not in any way want to denigrate or to diminish our achievements, because I do believe that all sections have benefited and that freedom has made a difference even to the person who is living in the remotest area—with all this, we find that disparities have increased. To some extent it was inevitable but I think to some extent it was preventable.

The Congress may believe in socialism. But do we not have people amongst us who have decried socialism publicly and privately? The

*Speech to the All-India Congress Committee at Bangalore, July 12, 1969.

Congress has stood in the international field for non-alignment. But do we not have people amongst us who have decried non-alignment publicly and privately? The Congress has stood for the eradication of untouchability but even in this sphere can we say that everyone of our members is behind this programme? I am giving you a few examples. It is not that we do not have a good programme before us. It may not also be that the Congress as a party does not support these projects. But what have we done to make these programmes real—not just to the public, but real to our own members?

If they decry our policies, it is obviously because they have not understood them or because they do not stand for that for which India has stood and the Congress has stood throughout its history.

Ours is an ancient country with a very rich heritage. Many of our ideals are old ideals. Gandhiji did not say anything new when he said that Truth is good. And yet how many of his speeches Gandhiji devoted just to this one subject, stressing the necessity of truth, of co-operation, of working together, of equality between sections of the people? None of these things were new for our country or for any country. Yet they were repeated day after day by Gandhiji in his prayer meetings because there was need for such repetition.

Today there is very great need for the A.I.C.C. to reiterate our basic ideas and our basic policies. Where do we want to go? We want to eradicate poverty. The capitalist system says it wants to eradicate poverty, and the communist system also says that it wants to eradicate poverty. But we have not adopted any of these systems because we find that they have not worked in their own country, and they have had to pay a tremendous price. That is why we chose another way.

I was very sad yesterday that one of our members here cast some aspersions that some of the leaders, perhaps meaning me, wanted to encourage the Communists. Now, nobody who is interested in the freedom of his country—freedom in the sense in which we understand it, that is, not merely political freedom, but freedom of expression and so many other freedoms—can ever be Communist. Our fight with the Communists is not just that it is a Communist Party or that the word Communist is there. I am not allergic to that word. But I am allergic to some of their ideas and to some of their methods. And I am allergic to anybody who uses that method. In India it is not only the Communists who are using it.

In all these long speeches, we did not hear a word of condemnation for the communal riots which are taking place. Did anybody draw attention to the fact that we, after all these years, with all our great desire for secularism, which is one of the pillars of our domestic policy, have not been able to control the situation, that little by little we are losing the trust of the minority? Why is it so? It is because we talk about those things and we think that our task is finished after talking about them.

In nearly every A.I.C.C. meeting, I have taken up the question of a cadre because it is not enough to say this is our policy. We must have people who are dedicating their entire time to spreading our ideas and to converting people. No political party exists merely in itself. It has to grow or it atrophies little by little. I do not say for a minute that Congress is atrophying. I think it is dynamic. It has strength. But I do not think that it is growing at the pace which our nation requires, even at the pace at which the growing population of India requires.

Do we have the trust of the young people? Do we have the trust of the intellectuals? Do we have the entire trust of any section? If we go to one group they think we are with the other group. If we go to the other group they think that we are with a third group. Why have these doubts arisen? To some extent, it is true, because we criticise ourselves. We say many things ourselves and these are exaggerated and exploited. This should not be ignored. But the fact remains that as of today we do not make that kind of impact on the public which makes them say: "This is a socialistic party. This is a party which with all its strength is going out to achieve certain ends."

I feel that we shall not exist long if we do not convert ourselves into such a path. What gave strength to us was that whenever we drifted a little from the main path, Gandhiji brought us back and said: "Well, all that is good but the real thing is this." Now we tend to drift from the real thing. We have to work together and we have worked together. We have to compromise and many times we have compromised. But should the compromise be on any basic principle? The basic principle and policies are commitment and deep involvement with socialist policy, and commitment and deep involvement with the policy of secularism.

We fought for freedom and the momentum and the energy that were generated in that struggle took us to freedom, and freedom spread all over the country. In some way, even though the freedom struggle had been going on for long, we took those who dominated us somewhat by surprise. But after all these years, these nations have recovered from their surprise and we see the same old struggle going on in the world for influencing other nations. It is much cheaper to influence a nation from outside than to have your Government there. You get all the benefit without any of the trouble. This is the world situation today. I have not been very happy with the words Left and Right because I think in themselves they have no meaning. Left of what? Right of what? Just like people have been calling that portion of the world where the Arab countries are as the Middle East. Middle from where? If we look at it from India, certainly it is not the Middle East. It is far to our West. And that is why we started calling it West Asia, because no matter from which side you look at the map that area is always West Asia.

But people, when they use such terms as Left and Right which cannot be well defined, naturally give them their own meaning. Many of us tend to look at our problems not from the eyes of the Indian but from the eyes of whichever people we admire or who are able to influence us for the moment. We see Indian progress measured by the yardstick of some of the advanced countries. We see Indian progress measured by the yardstick of very small countries which have been recipients of tremendous aid from outside. But Indian problems have to be viewed in the context of the Indian situation. That is why, keeping that in view, we chose the path of democracy, secularism and socialism in the domestic sphere, and what we called non-alignment in the international sphere.

And no matter what way we look at the situation, that situation has not changed, neither in India nor in the world. One member came to me just before the A.I.C.C. and said that now that there was a little more prosperity in India, people would not want socialism because as they get more they tended to become more conservative. It is true that once a person has something, he is anxious to keep it and he is not anxious for big changes. But in India the vast majority of people do not have anything that they can keep at the moment. We talk of freedom but there still are people whose freedom is extremely limited, because when you do not get enough of your basic necessities you cannot be fully free to think or to express yourselves or to do what you like. This was the basic problem before us and we consciously took the middle way. We had a private sector and we started a public sector. I think all of you will agree that the private sector has benefited since Independence. There has been expansion of their industries, expansion of their trade, expansion of their business. How much richer they have grown! And yet not for one day have they appreciated the policy of the Government. There is a constant struggle that the private sector must be much bigger. There is constant criticism that the public sector is not working well. Even on this platform I heard some people say yesterday what tremendous losses are being made by the public sector. Now, I do not have all the figures here, and I do not want to go into them, but I think all of you ought to go into the question. The members of the A.I.C.C. should certainly take this matter seriously. There are losses, we don't want to deny them, but there are profits also. Not all the public sector is incurring a loss. Not all the private sector is working without any blemish. In fact, more and more demands are coming that perhaps the whole matter should be looked into. And perhaps it will be looked into.

So the struggle is not of words, it is something very much deeper. It is not a struggle that has begun today. It is a struggle which has been there from the very first day that we used the word socialism for our policy. It went on all the time while my father was there. We did pass resolutions for the reason perhaps that the public would like them, because perhaps the majority of the members would like them, but we did not act upon the resolutions, because those who did not wish to act upon them were able to pull their strength.

In a democratic organisation, any group should certainly be able to pull its weight. If anybody feels this policy is not the right policy, he has the full right to change that policy, to modify it, to adapt it or to do what he likes. But, as I said, there is one factor which has to be considered, and that is the needs of the Indian people, and the feelings of the Indian people. When we talk of the people, each of us talks of that section which he or she knows best. If somebody is in business, when he says "people" he means business people. If somebody happens to be a legal person, when he says "people" he thinks of the law people. It is right, because you know those people best. But the vast mass of the people do not belong to any of these groups. They belong to sections who, in spite of all the political consciousness, in spite of all our efforts, in spite of mass adult franchise in elections, still have no voice. We saw in the last election how in some places people were not allowed to vote as they wanted to vote. So this is a struggle between the strong and the weak.

This is nothing new. Tagore wrote about it long before Independence. Many others have written about it. But Tagore also wrote that the strong should never underestimate the strength of the weak, because in any country the weakness of any section pulls down the whole country. In an article which he wrote, he has likened the strong to an elephant and the weak to quicksand. When the elephant gets caught in quicksand, with all its strength it cannot be saved.

What are the conditions in the country today? Are they not somewhat like quicksand? However strong the Congress organisation is in itself, low long can it withstand this quicksand? There are other parties. There are parties which are not behaving perhaps in the democratic way. Some of our people have suggested that they should be banned. There has been a slogan for banning of the Jana Sangh. Earlier there has been a slogan for the banning of the Communist party. But if the problem which they have created remains, then merely banning a party is not going to solve it for you. You have to tackle that problem and that problem can be tackled only organisationally. This is why, again and again, we come back to the question of how solid is our organisation. When we have talked of bogus membership we are told that it is impossible to remove it. Now if any organisation has a large element of bogus membership, is that strength? Is it worthwhile having a long list of names when we do not know whose names they are? Is it not better to have names from which we can know that he or she is doing such and such a work, and that he or she can influence that area or can do something. We have been a party based on constructive work in the wider perspective on social and economic change. But what do we see now? We see that we are mostly concerned with elections. In between it is true that when there is a natural calamity the Congress comes forward. I must congratulate our members on the way they respond magnificently. Ours is the only party which really goes out and takes up such challenge—whether it is floods or earthquake or drought or anything like that. Otherwise they think that there is nothing to be done.

So, when I jotted down these points the question was not whether they are new points or old points. It was not even whether all these things can be done immediately. The consideration was only this, that every now and then we must restate what we stand for. Every now and then we must have the opportunity of seeing our goal and judging how far we have gone along the path.

I have the privilege of belonging to the Congress even when I was not a member. I regarded myself as a member of the Congress from the day when I hardly walked. So it is certainly not my intention ever to do anything that would weaken this great organisation. But with all my love and my pride in the Congress organisation, I must say that there is something which is bigger than the Congress and that is our country and that is our people (applause). And the day we forget that and we talk only about our party, that day will see the weakening of the party. This is what we should remember when we gather at the A.I.C.C. It is not a fight of personalities. We may feel that a certain thing should have been said or unsaid or said in one way or another way. These are not the relevant points. The only relevant point is whether we really feel that we are in touch with the people who are willing to deal with their problems. We can honestly say this only to ourselves, not even to our next-door neighbour.

Some agitation takes place. And if we find that we can get something out of it, we are not concerned whether that agitation is in the long run bad for the country or good, we jump into it full-heartedly. If a demand is made, we do not stop to consider whether the demand should really be fulfilled, what the difficulties are, whether we should go to the people and tell them that we cannot do this. No, we say that this is a popular demand therefore we must have it. We hasten to be in the forefront of that demand. So we are all the time creating conditions in which it becomes more difficult for us to work. Gandhiji constantly talked about service and sacrifice. But this is what it adds up to, the courage to face up to a situation and not see whether this is going to get us something or not, but ask: Is it the right thing to do? My experience has been that in whatever part of India, whenever we have faced up to a problem we have not only had the strength to face up to it, but we have also had success.

There is talk of unity. Certainly there should be unity. I have on every occasion talked of unity and worked for unity. But again unity for what? Is that unity strong unity, which is going to strengthen the organisation, which is going to take us ahead? Or is it a unity in which we say, merely for the sake of being together: "Let us forget our ideals. It does not matter if we are going in the right direction or not." These are some of the problems which have to be faced. We face them today, or face them tomorrow, or face them after some time. You must be aware of these problems and my whole purpose in sending this note was to draw attention to the basic problems. Had I known that this note was going to be put before the A.I.C.C., I can tell you I would have sent an entirely different type of note which would have been far more comprehensive. In the present note, many things which I consider equally important have been left out. Some of them were touched upon in the note produced by Shri Sadiq Ali and Shri Subramaniam, and some other matters had also been put in, by others. And I had thought that that was the note which was going before you here. So I did not say anything about that note in what I wrote but just jotted down some of the basic things which I thought should be considered. With the result I find that their note has been completely ignored and I must say that I am sorry about this, because it has some very valuable ideas and some programmes which we should consider and implement.

There is constant talk about the lack of money. I know that there are many programmes and projects which have to be taken up but which we cannot just now take up for lack of money. But we can make a beginning, not only as Government, but as a party, as a people. Everywhere, in villages and so on, there still is a great response if you take up something earnestly. But we as a party take the same stand as the public takes and say: "This is Government's business." The Government cannot shrug off its responsibility. But everywhere in the world, the party's business is to support the Government. And by support I do not mean just voting. Support means to do what you can do in promoting programmes, in promoting ideology, and in fighting against all that stands opposed to the programmes and the ideology.

As a nation and a people we have been committed to very high ideals. It is not possible for us to live up to those ideals all the time. But we must keep them before us all the time. I spoke earlier about some of the difficulties which the countries which have become independent now face. Because we are going ahead, we tend to forget the many dangers which threaten us inside and outside the country. But those dangers are very real and are growing. We have to recognise them and we have to face up to them. The Congress has always stood for real independence in foreign policy. We chose the word non-alignment to describe it, but the word does not, I am afraid, give the full meaning of our policy. The meaning only was that to have a free and an independent foreign policy, we have to be independent of any bloc of any other countries outside. This is the road along which we have been going. I think it is important to mention it here, because it is important for the A.I.C.C. to decide whether it wants to go along that road or whether it thinks that we cannot go along that road and we should align ourselves with one or the other bloc. Some of our policies have been denigrated at a most peculiar time, at a time when other nations are applauding them, when other nations are coming round to our point of view, those who thought that the policies were against them. We try to give things a personal twist. We try to put labels on people. I am against all this. No person can be a container of pickles or something that can be put in a bottle and labelled! "So and so is so and so." We are vital, changing, human beings.

Why have other parties made progress? Have we made any effort to see that the process is halted? Have we done some ground-work so that in future we should have a say? Are we looking into the problems which these parties have raised? Obviously they were somehow able to get a foothold in the people. It cannot be only by wrongdoing. Wrongdoing does help sometimes. If you terrorize the people, perhaps you can get something done. But not for very long. Along with it if you have done something which the people need, then you get a chance to exploit the situation and strengthen yourself by other means as well. Why do we not look into what these other parties have done and see what has to be done?

This is one of my objects when I say that the major problems before us are: one, land reform, and two, the question of unemployment. These are two questions which we have to look at very seriously. We cannot solve them overnight or even in a year. But if we give the people an impression that we are serious about solving them, then we also have our foothold. Otherwise little by little we shall lose our place with the people and we shall be a party that is linked with some group not with the masses at large. Again and again I am calling attention to this, because it is something which we speak about but which is no longer in our hearts. We look at it from the intellectual point of view, but that is not enough. We have to be involved in it in our hearts. We have to do this regardless of the fact whether we win or lose. We have to work for what we consider is right regardless of the fact of what it does to us. Only then we shall have the strength to work for it. If we are working for it only from the point of view that this will get us something immediately, then we do not get the basic thing and we also lose what you think you are going to get. I think this has happened in many places to Congress Governments. We have not dared to criticise certain wrong things, for instance communal riots. We have not met up to the challenge of the Jana Sangh. Some people have said: "Why don't we combine with other democratic parties?" They think that the Jana Sangh is a democratic party. Is that their idea of democracy that some people in the country should be of lesser stature than others? Which is the democratic party with whom we could combine? Although we claim we do not want opportunistic alliances, we talk in a way which does not sound convincing. I have no doubt that this talk has weakened the Congress as a whole. If we go along our path and stick to our basic policies, I do not say we shall not be defeated once or twice or in this or that part of India, but I have no doubt that in the long run we shall succeed, we shall come out on top. And even if we do not come out on top, if by our right doing we have advanced the country one step in that direction, I say that that is a far bigger success than winning any election or being in power. But I must confess that this kind of spirit has gone from our organisation. I am not blaming any person, because I am equally involved and all of us who are members of the Congress are involved. We think always in terms of groups. We think we are in a group. We think other people are also in a group, and an atmosphere of suspicion, of mistrust, and a lot of in-fighting is created. We know that this in-fighting has lost us elections in many places. But basically why do all these things happen? Because of going away from the basic path.

If you are seriously involved in something, you will not allow your effort to be weakened. This is what happened when we were involved in the freedom struggle. Even then there was some in-fighting. Not everybody was together. There was the same kind of group rivalry, political rivalry, personal rivalry. All these things existed, but because of the deep and sincere involvement in the freedom struggle, those things always got abated. And that is how we could win freedom. If today we can keep our involvement with the people of India, and refuse to dilute our basic policies even by a little, then I think success is assured.

There was much talk here on the nationalisation of banks. That was the main bone of contention. As I have said earlier, mere nationalisation will make no difference. And with all due respect I would say that I do not think that even removing industrialists and putting bankers makes any difference. It does not matter if the person is an industrialist, a banker or a peasant or a businessman. What matters is what his ideology is. Does he believe in what we want to do? That is the question. What his profession is is immaterial. What his wealth is is quite immaterial. The people whom we are putting in charge of various things, are they committed to our programme? I must say that by and large they are not. Why are the public sector projects not flourishing as they should? Because the people in charge of them are not people who are committed to the public sector. By nationalisation I am certainly not for some kind of bureaucratic regime or State Capitalism or that kind of thing. We must have people who have the right ideas, who are not in it for the sake of a job, who are not in it just to do something, but who are deeply committed to the basic objective. Whether it is a bank, whether it is industry, whether it is an agricultural programme, the end is not that but something else. The end is what that programme will ultimately do for the people.

For instance, there is a farmers' lobby in our party. It is good for the farmers to have a lobby. They are a very important section of the population. But the farmers' lobby ignores the vast numbers of the landless, the vast number of those smaller farmers who have no lobby, who have no voice, who have no organisation. Can we afford to be separated from those people?

It was rightly said that we cannot today measure a country's progress by the gross national product. A high rate of growth is not sufficient for a country like India. Even if it is increased, there are large sections who are untouched by that growth. That growth by itself sows the seeds of tension, of agitation and of ill-will. So this is the basic question before the A.I.C.C. —not just what programme we are taking up but in what spirit are we doing it. And how much we are prepared to sacrifice for the sake of that right spirit, for the sake of the right method. It cannot be done without sacrifice. Every step forward touches some interest. It may touch the farmers' interest. It may touch the industrialists' interest. And that lobby is immediately active against us. We have seen it in our press, we have seen it in a hundred and one ways, how pressures are brought to bear upon us. It is very easy to give in to the pressure. But then, as I said, you have the greater danger of alienating yourself from the mass of the people.

The spirit in which this resolution was put here is that we should rededicate ourselves to our basic socialist policies, we should rededicate ourselves to a spirit of service and sacrifice, and not give in to the calculation of what will help us at this moment or the next moment. Personalities are not important. We have had some of the greatest personalities in our organisation but they always drew their strength from the people. And they said so.

The question is how strong we want the Congress to be, how strong we want India to be. Today no other country is interested in India being strong. They would all want to help us to some extent, that is all. Beyond that they would not like a country with a large population like India, a large land mass like India, to be really and effectively strong. That burden is only on us. And therefore we have in all these problems to mark out a road, which may not perhaps be approved by everybody but which we know in our hearts is the right road for our people. I hope that the Congress Party will always keep to this road and to this manner of progress, and not be enticed by the glitter of any other path that other countries are taking. When you look at some of the modernisation which is taking place in many countries, you ask yourselves: wealth is increasing, but what wealth? Of acquisition and of glitter rather than of substance. Is that the path which India wants to take? No. That would be fatal, a disaster.

These are some of the matters which we have to consider in great seriousness. Sometimes we take up a slogan—now it is Bank Nationalisation. It may be a good thing; is may not be. But it has become a slogan; somehow it is identified with the essence of radicalism. That to my mind is going away from the main point. You may believe in it; you may do it. I am not saying do not do it. But it is not right to cling to anything as a slogan and to say that that is the only thing. At all times these slogans must be put in the perspective of the larger good of the country.

I spoke earlier of the struggle, in the world, of spheres of influence and so on. India has been playing a very important, though purposely inconspicuous, role in many areas. We believe that the stand we have taken, although it has brought us criticism quite often, has ultimately convinced people that we stand firm on our idea. That is why India's voice is heeded in the world's councils even today. Some people feel it would have been simpler if we had said all this is not our business and why should we interfere? But we said it was our interest, because our leaders from the beginning said "Freedom is indivisible, progress is indivisible and if there is lack of freedom anywhere it adversely influences the rest of the world. As freedom grows, other countries which are not free also get the strength and the courage."

The situation is exactly the same within the country. Do we have the strength to strike out on our own? I believe Congress has the dynamism; it has the programme, it has the policy, it has the achievement which can give it the strength in the eyes of the people. But we do still lack the capacity to project this image. Why should there be doubt about these things? Can we in the A.I.C.C. see that we will resolve to remove these doubts from the minds of the public? So this is something which all of us must resolve if we want the Congress to be what it was in the past, that is a party with a mass base which is committed to the people of India, and a party which does not mind even if it is not there for power, which is not there for success, but which is there for an ideal, the ideal of giving economic and social content to freedom, the ideal of raising all those sections of the people who have been under-privileged, who have been oppressed, and who are even today suffering from injustice. This is what we must resolve.

Just before coming here, I happened to see a film which is a part of the film which is made on Gandhiji's life from real photographs and films taken at that time. And in the part I saw, he was telling people that they must keep a diary of their daily work, so that they know that they had achieved something each day. I do not know if it is necessary to keep a daily diary, but certainly there must be some way of judging what work each person has done and in which direction. Only then can you know whether the programme which we have taken up is being followed or not. Only when we are ourselves convinced can we convince other people.

Therefore let us work together for a strong and united party, and for a unity which is based on policy—on real belief in the ideals which our leaders have put before us. Then we can convince everybody of our capacity to put them into action. We have come to one of the most beautiful parts of India, a state which has made good progress, and where progress is visible. But it needs to be shown that the progress is not only in outward view but also in the thinking of the people. The people should realise that this direction is a right direction, although the pace may not always be what they expect. They should be convinced that we always keep the people's interest in the forefront and the party's interest second, and groups, personalities and so on after that. This should be the message of the Bangalore Congress. And I am sure that if we can go back with this message and see that we work it out then the Congress will indeed have a brighter future.

3. OPEN LETTER TO MEMBERS OF THE CONGRESS PARTY*

Dear Colleague,

There is a crisis in the Congress and in the nation.

It is not a crisis which has come about all of a sudden. It has been building over a long time.

What we witness today is not a mere clash of personalities, and certainly not a fight for power. It is not as simple as a conflict between the parliamentary and organisational wings.

It is a conflict between two outlooks and attitudes in regard to the objectives of the Congress and the methods by which the Congress itself should function.

It is a conflict between those who are for socialism, for change and for the fullest internal democracy and debate in the organisation on the one hand, and those who are for the status quo, for conformism and for less than full discussion inside the Congress.

Even if some good people are in the second group, this basic analysis is not affected. An individual here or there not sharing the outlook of the group does not alter the basic facts of the situation.

The Congress stands for democracy, secularism, socialism and non-alignment in international relations.

The various policy-making units of our organisation, whether the Working Committee, or the A.I.C.C. or the delegates' session, have re-affirmed these objectives from time to time. But within the Congress there has been a group which did not have total faith in these objectives. People of this group paid only lip service to these ideals because they knew that if they openly expressed their reservations they would lose the power and influence they had derived from the party.

This group is not a new phenomenon. It has existed in our party throughout the last twenty-two years and even before. I know that this group constantly tried to check and frustrate my father's attempt to bring about far-reaching economic and social changes. The Congress was moulded by Mahatma Gandhi and my father to be the prime instrument

*Written on November 18, 1969.

of social change. The acceptance of office and of responsibilities of government was, after all, to bring about this non-violent revolution in our society. If this cannot be done, what is the use of Congress or what is the purpose of being in Government?

In his last years, my father was greatly concerned that the Congress was moving away from the people and that there were persons inside the Congress who were offering resistance to change. My own experience even before the fourth general election was that the forces of status quo, with close links with powerful economic interests, were ranged against me.

While the biggest leaders of the Congress were involved in the tasks of government and administration in the years after freedom, some persons developed a vested interest in power. They began to regard themselves as the Congress, forgetting that they could keep their mandate only through service and only if the Congress had a powerful mass base. To consolidate their hold and in the name of discipline they pushed out of the Congress many honest and devoted workers, whose loyalty to the organisation and its ideals was beyond question. Their arrogant use of authority made some people resign from the Congress or retire from active work. It also discouraged fresh streams of young workers from flowing into the Congress. The worker in the field was denied his right to mould the party and the party registers were packed with bogus names. Recently the tendency to acquire factional control of the organisation has become more intense. This is linked up with the desire to control the direction of Government policy and economic life in line with the narrow purposes and interests of a limited section.

This is the background to the present crisis. As I recently told the Bombay Pradesh Congress workers, some of those who are now worried about a split remained complacent when the strength of the Congress was being wilfully sacrificed in State after State and in election after election.

The time has come to bring all this into the open, so that there might be full and free discussion of the problems of the Congress. I do not want a split in our great national organisation, which brought freedom to our country and which has to fulfil its promise by building a new society. But I want unity which is a unity on principles and on methods of work. To speak of socialism and secularism, to vote for them in meetings, but to have a public image of association with those who are opposed to secularism and socialism is no service to the Congress.

The full details of the present crisis are well known to all of you.

The correspondence fully brings out the background of the requisition which the majority of the A.I.C.C. members presented to the Congress Working Committee and which was so summarily, unconstitutionally and unwisely turned down.

As you know, certain Chief Ministers strove to bring about a compromise but even while they were continuing their efforts, Shri Nijalingappa asked me to explain my "conduct". Even after this notice was served, I met Shri Nijalingappa and discussed with him certain proposals on which Shri K. C. Abraham and Shri Veerendra Patil had worked.

Since Shri Nijalingappa, for whose personal qualities I have high regard, had felt that requisition was a vote of censure on him, inasmuch as it was confined to the Congress President's election and left out other elections, I suggested that we might have a new election to all elected offices above the P.C.C. level as an interim measure, pending the revision of rolls and new elections at all levels on the basis of rolls which were cleansed of bogus membership.

Shri Nijalingappa on the contrary spoke of taking up the whole process of election on the basis of the existing rolls which is obviously no answer to the crisis since it would retard the remedial action that can still be taken to set things right in the organisation.

Even as regards this proposal, unsatisfactory as it was, Shri Nijalingappa made no firm commitment. He only said that any written proposal which was made to him would be placed before the Working Committee. He did not vouchsafe any information on whether the meeting would be that of the truncated body or of the full body. I did not discuss the 'show cause' notice with him and he did not offer to rescind it. From other reliable sources it was learnt that he had every intention of taking action against me and others.

To go back from these details to the main question of the crisis before the country. Outside the narrow confines of our Party, great and turbulent changes are taking place in the minds and hearts of our people. There are new trends of thought. There are new aspirations. And there are new tensions apart from some other older tensions. Political consciousness has matured and deepened among the masses and in this process, many ideas, some old and some new, are being canvassed, and a kind of crystallisation has been steadily taking place.

Faced with this change in the national political environment, our party has been in danger of losing its orientation; it has been trying to cope with the situation by a ritualistic repetition of the formal positions of the past without making a fresh assessment of the needs of the present and the future in accordance with its own living revolutionary tradition.

There is a loss of confidence in ourselves and in the destiny both of our country and of our party. There is a tendency to be influenced by the forces of reaction, revivalism and vested interests.

In this situation, it is necessary for the Congress to recognise frankly that it no longer commands in full the loyalty and emotions of the nation as it did in the past. It must also recognise that it cannot discharge the role of leadership unless it re-defines its position sharply in relation to the competing points of view in the country; and it can serve as an effective instrument of the national purpose only if it revitalises its membership and its methods of functioning.

The Congress must open its closed doors to winds of change, re-establish its living links with the people in every town and village of India. It must make a fresh effort to forge fresh links with the new generation which has grown since our independence. It must reflect the modern elements in our society. It must draw unto itself the live elements of modern science and technology. It must command the loyalty of our intelligentsia. It must seek to induce amongst the ordinary people a feeling of confidence that we are a party which seeks to serve the people.

In the nature of things, a national debate on the issues at stake and the competing points of view cannot be carried on without some pain and emotional disturbance. But the need for the debate is inescapable. No one can stifle it. Indeed, effective political leadership lies in promoting an orderly, sober, civilised discussion of the issues we have to resolve. We cannot treat a fresh debate as the sign of a revolt against any individual or group. The subversion of free debate constitutes a danger to democracy not only within our Party, but in the country.

The basic issue in the conflict must be separated from other issues which, though important, are secondary. That basic issue is whether the democratic process shall prevail or not in the Congress.

There are legal and constitutional aspects of the conflict. These have been discussed fully in the correspondence that has passed between me and Mr. Nijalingappa. The legal and constitutional issues are important. But behind them is the far more important issue whether Congressmen who have built the Congress at great sacrifice are to run it and mould it as they like or whether bosses should run it as they like. There has been always a conflict between bossism and democracy, and it is this conflict which has reached a critical stage.

The aim of the Congress still is to bring about far-reaching social and economic change amounting to a social revolution. But it has ceased to be a fit instrument of its own aims and is losing its sense of purpose. It has been losing its articulation, its sense of direction, and its old confidence. The average Congressman has been denied his voice in it, and the committees at various levels are hardly functioning.

The present conflict, or debate, or whatever else it is called, concerns what the Congress can still do for the people. It is wedded to democratic socialism. Both democracy and socialism are necessary. Without the one, the other cannot exist. Democracy is inevitable in the conditions of this country; so is socialism. The democratic process and the socialist process can go together. Indian experience has proved it, and we must take the two processes together. The Congress, as the most broad-based organisation, can do it best. That is why it has always to keep its goal of socialism in view and maintain the democratic process within itself.

There is no place for a sectarian approach. Socialism in this country can come about only as the result of an open, broad movement. It cannot come overnight. Both the Government and the people must work for it. The people must be mobilised in support of socialist measures undertaken by the Government. Legislation alone is not enough.

The organisation is important to mobilise the people for socialism. It is not enough for it to come to life only for elections. It must be constantly at work to educate the people regarding our policies and actions. Social power has to be organised in support of political power. This social power is necessary even to win elections. The organisation cannot afford to become weak in any part. It must be ever vigilant and active. Even with its recent amendments, the Constitution is still inadequate for the requirements of the fast changing situation. The desire to immediately change the set-up even to a limited extent, arises because of the necessity to consider in depth in what manner further radical transformation of the organisation can be brought about. The membership must be real, not artificial. The commitment must be sincere. There must be a sense of urgency.

The Government is a part of the organisation. If the organisation is live, the Government will be aware of its responsibility. The state of the organisation is reflected in the legislative parties and the Government.

There is no conflict between the two wings. The relations between them have often been discussed and are well understood.

The importance of the organisation cannot be minimised. To make it real and alive and to make it work democratically, and dynamically, is the aim of the meeting of the members of the A.I.C.C. that will be held in Delhi. It can release vast energies, and these energies can take the Congress and the people forward.

CHAPTER SIX

Foreign Policy and the United Nations

1. UN CONFERENCE ON TRADE AND DEVELOPMENT, 1968*

I AM GLAD YOU HAVE CHOSEN THIS COUNTRY FOR YOUR DELIBER-
ATIONS. Here you will find the problems which all struggling nations face,
and you will see them, if I may say so, projected on a giant screen. You
will see them not as statistics but in the expectant glances of our bright-
eyed young people and in the anxious faces of their elders. We are conscious that we bear the mark of the storms we have weathered. I hope
you will also recognise the spirit of the country, a spirit which has seen
our people through countless difficulties, natural calamities, man-made
complexities. It is this spirit which has inspired our great men through the
ages. Some of our problems are centuries old, and some are very new—
parched land and bursting cities, illiteracy and brain drain.

For more than a hundred years, the most sensitive and perceptive minds
in our country have been obsessed with poverty and have striven to
remove its causes. Our fight for freedom was itself part of the greater
fight to liberate our people from the grip of poverty and the fear of
economic insecurity. The vastness of our country makes the challenge so
much the greater. Whatever we do, must be done for 560,000 villages. In
the last fifteen years, we have almost doubled agricultural production,
created 30 million jobs, put 45 million more children in schools, added 20
years to the life-span, and established a base of heavy industries, but we
cannot even take time off to think of this as an achievement. We must go
on with our work, for what is unfinished is so much larger than what is
done.

In our unending labour, our consolation is that we are not alone.

*Address inaugurating the Second United Nations Conference on Trade and Development,
New Delhi, February 1, 1968.

Through the long hard struggle for political independence, we were keenly aware of other nations and of peoples who also were oppressed by their fellow-men. We shared with them the indignities and humiliations of discrimination and exploitation,—of this was forged a kinship. It has been our hope and constant endeavour that India should work not only for herself but for the larger world community. At the greatest moment of our lives, when we became free and sovereign, my father pledged us to the service of India. He said,

> The service of India means the service of the millions who suffer. It means the ending of poverty and ignorance and disease and inequality of opportunity . . . And so we have to labour and to work, and work hard, to give reality to our dreams. Those dreams are for India, but they are also for the world, for, all nations and peoples are too closely knit together today, for any one of them to imagine that it can live apart. Peace has been said to be indivisible, so is freedom, so is prosperity now, and so also is disaster in this One World that can no longer be split into isolated fragments.

The United Nations was established twenty-three years ago to keep world peace and promote human prosperity. The juxtaposition of peace and prosperity is not a contrivance for stating moral precepts. The two are indissolubly linked together. Without peace there can be no prosperity for any people, rich or poor. And yet, there can be no peace without erasing the harshness of the growing contrast between the rich and the poor. Unless we sense this urgency and use our energy to eradicate the economic causes which make for conflict, men and women will be impelled to revolt, and to use violent means to bring about change.

Wherever a wide gulf has divided the small section of the rich from the vast masses of the poor, the State has either imposed a forced peace on the opposing camps or faced instability from within. What has been true within a nation is equally valid for the international community. Apart from reducing the inequalities within their social structures, the developing nations must adopt modern technology to create a new balance of benefit to all their citizens. In this endeavour, can we not apply to the problems of the world community the accumulated experience of some of the member States of the United Nations who are now in the vanguard of progress? Can we not co-operate to give meaning and substance to the very concept of a world community? These are the questions before this Conference.

This is not the first occasion for the United Nations to address itself to the problems of world poverty and hunger. The Charter of this great Organisation calls upon it to work for the removal of want. To achieve this objective, a number of international organisations were set up. In December 1961, the General Assembly declared the Sixties as the Decade of Development. In June 1964, the first UN Conference on Trade and Development adopted its Final Act, a blueprint drawn up to achieve a better balance in international economic relationships. But we find that concrete action has fallen far short of its declaration. In the meantime, year by year, the needs of the developing nations are becoming more acute, more urgent.

Some success has of course been achieved. Funds raised by diverse methods have been invested in the process of development. Difficulties have been studied in depth, and the continuing machinery of this Conference has been engaged in a search for solutions. Under the able guidance of its distinguished Secretary-General, the Secretariat has produced valuable documents which I am sure you will find useful. The Group of '77' has even prepared a modest though practical programme of action. Naturally, hope is reawakened by the presence of so many distinguished statesmen from different parts of the world. But we are also haunted by the fear that the historic opportunity to set the world community firmly on the road to peace and prosperity might again be missed.

Are these fears altogether groundless? The Development Decade is drawing to a close. During the last years, most Member States have laboured, individually or collectively, to promote economic advancement in underdeveloped countries. An average growth rate of 4·6 per cent per annum has been achieved, but it dwindles to a mere 2 per cent, if we take into account the increases in population. Anyhow, the average growth rate is at best an imperfect measure of social and economic development. A much surer guide is the per capita income, on which the efforts so far made have had little impact. It is the human aspect—the opportunity for men and women everywhere to lead a fuller life—which is of the utmost importance. So long as the fundamental rights of millions of people in regard to employment, food, shelter and other needs remain unsatisfied, so long will their urge to rise to their full stature and serve their fellow men remain unfulfilled.

The situation is a source of anxiety. The goal is distant. But impatience and dissatisfaction sap our will to persevere. Those who look upon development assistance as repayable charity will inevitably miss the expected gratitude from its beneficiaries. Those who view it as investment to earn political support or to collect dividends or to promote trade will be disappointed with the meagre returns. At the same time, growing numbers in the developing countries are beginning to look upon external capital and know-how, not as aids to their own strength and achievement of economic freedom, but as bonds which increase their dependence on dominant economies. We must all plead guilty to being tempted by the illusion that small efforts can yield big results. This is why we become disenchanted, and international economic co-operation is the first casualty. Thus, domestic pressures mount. Our affluent friends seek to curtail their contribution to development. In turn the recipients of aid retreat inwards.

Sovereign nations are gathered here. But in some cases the structure of their mutual economic relationship has been inherited from their colonial past. We are all familiar with the part colonialism has played in the exploitation of dependent countries. The dominant powers introduced modern science and industry to agricultural lands. But they developed only those segments of dependent economics which met metropolitan needs. They did not build the economic base for the development of material and human resources and of self-generating growth.

Today the rich nations find it more rewarding to invest their savings in their own security, in the advance of their technology, or even in establishing contacts with distant planets. They find it more interesting to trade amongst themselves than with the developing nations. Their markets and profit patterns are protected by tariff and non-tariff barriers. The efforts of the less developed countries to process their natural products and increase their share of international trade in manufactured and processed goods are thus frustrated. The continuous onslaught of synthetics and substitutes further deprives poor nations of the resources they could derive from the use of their products.

Thus, the gap keeps growing. The technological and scientific advances achieved by industrial nations accelerate this process. While industrial nations naturally use their resources to improve their technology, developing nations do not have even the means to borrow it. Even so, modern technology offers to the developing nations the possibility of avoiding the earlier stages of development and thus overcoming the challenge of poverty.

How can this possibility be realised? How can nations now embarking on the difficult task of modernising their economies be helped to tele- scope their industrial effort—spread over two to three generations in most advanced countries—into a decade or two? How can they mobilise the immense capital needed for investment in developmental projects, while making at least some provision for social welfare? How long can the hope of a minimum improvement in the standard of personal consumption be postponed, when the people are so conscious of their rights as well as of the grim realities of their comparative situation? How can economic activities meet the requirements of efficiency and be geared to the achieve- ment of rapid advance, while ensuring the dignity of the human being and guaranteeing to the individual full enjoyment of his fundamental rights?

These conflicts cannot be resolved in a day or even in a decade. Their solution demands patience, understanding, right motivation, and above all, a far greater effort and bigger sacrifice than we have so far volunteered. Poverty corrodes the spirit of the poor and weakens their will to over- come it. The wealth of the prosperous grows in isolation and does not provide support to those who need it. The world economy has no built-in corrective. Economic processes must therefore be guided by a moral pur- pose and directed towards desirable ends by the political will of the international community. Otherwise only those nations which have in- herited economic advantage from historical accidents can hope to achieve the maximum gains within the area of their political control.

Responsibility for development must primarily be shouldered by the developing nations themselves. Political domination over the process of development by nations which wield economic power is inconsistent with the provisions of the Charter to which we all subscribe. What we need is a global strategy of development, an integrated programme of inter- national co-operation, which outlines convergent measures to be under- taken by every Member State. The elimination of poverty and the develop- ment of impoverished regions are now widely accepted as international obligations. In order to discharge them, it is imperative that the inter- national community find ways and means to intervene effectively in defining the responsibility of economic power, in matching resources to needs, and in guiding economic forces towards progress and peace.

Distinguished delegates assembled here have the experience of the last seven years of the Development Decade to guide them in their deliberations. Seven years is too short a period for mankind to tire or despair in this unprecedented endeavour. On the contrary, any shortcomings and inadequacies should spur us to a bigger and bolder effort. Remember, millions of people hopefully await on your decisions—the growers of jute, copra and cocoa, the miners of manganese and tin, the spinners and the weavers, to mention only a few. Their future is at stake, their own livelihood and the lives of their children, as also the capacity of their governments to provide the base for development.

The consequences of failure are too terrible to contemplate. Years ago Rabindranath Tagore wrote,

Power has to be made secure not only against power, but also against weakness; for there lies the peril of its losing balance. The weak are as great a danger for the strong as quicksand for an elephant. They do not assist progress because they do not resist, they only drag down. The people who grow accustomed to wield absolute power over others are apt to forget that by so doing they generate an unseen force which some day rends that power into pieces.

The question before the advanced nations is not whether they can afford to help the developing nations, but whether they can afford not to do so.

Poverty cannot be the destiny of the majority of mankind. I believe we have the power and the wisdom to give all these people new hope. With this faith I inaugurate the Second Conference of the United Nations on Trade and Development.

2. UN GENERAL ASSEMBLY, 1968*

The United Nations is the trustee of the world's peace and represents the hopes of mankind. Its very existence gives a feeling of assurance that the justice of true causes can be brought fearlessly before the world. This Assembly and the agencies of the United Nations should, in all that they do, sustain those hopes and promote the causes of peace.

Seven years ago, India's first Prime Minister, Jawaharlal Nehru, addressed this Assembly. He was a believer in seeking areas of agreement and

*Address delivered at the General Assembly of the United Nations, October 14, 1968.

co-operation, and in enlarging them. He advocated before this Assembly a 'new approach to co-operation and the furtherance of the co-operative effort'. The Assembly accepted his suggestion of an International Co-operation Year. The United Nations also launched a Development Decade to promote greater economic co-operation between the rich and the poor nations. Two major international conferences on trade and development were held.

The interest shown by Member States in these moves aroused great expectations among the developing countries. We did not seek to share the power of the big powers. We did not ask that they deny any of their own people their needs in order to fulfil ours. We, who have had twenty years or less of freedom to work for our progress, did not expect miracles of sudden transformation. Only too well do we know how long and hard is the path of development. What we do expect is understanding of the intangible yearnings of peoples who have long been under foreign domination.

Unfortunately, economic co-operation has little progress to show. Nor has there been any notable advance in international co-operation in the political sphere. The reasons for this failure are obvious and many: Economic and military power continues to dominate politics. The carving out of spheres of influence still motivates policies and actions. The desire to mould other nations in the image of one's own inspires propaganda, sowing seeds of mistrust. Nations continue to place narrow national ends above the larger purpose of peace and universal security.

In India we have been powerfully conditioned by Mahatma Gandhi. We believe that the evolution of individuals and societies depends on the extent to which they exercise self-restraint and abjure the use of force. Jawaharlal Nehru, who combined in himself modern political thought and the basic teaching of Mahatma Gandhi, strove to bring about a new system of relations amongst nations. He was tireless in advocating peaceful co-existence. He believed that in a world rent by conflict, freedom not fear, faith not doubt, confidence not suspicion would lead to friendship amongst nations.

The concept was evoking some response among statesmen and nations, and there was a growing recognition that howsoever difficult it might seem peaceful co-existence alone could enable the post-war world to solve its disputes rationally. But this trend has received severe jolts.

Every now and then violence erupts. Sheer power seemingly prevails over principles, seeking obedience and demanding respect instead of commanding it. Indeed, those who have attempted to eschew the use of force have had to pay the price of restraint. And yet, the world is changing. Implicit faith in the efficacy of and unquestioning dependence on military alliances, as well as the rigidities of the bipolar world, are in a state of flux. Every nation, regardless of its size, is endeavouring to establish its own identity. This encourages the hope that despite obstacles the United Nations will be able to help all nations to live in peace and independence.

While there is search for a more equitable and humane world order, force continues to be used to attain political ends and to promote national or global interests. It is not my intention to deal with specific issues. Our views have been stated in this Assembly and elsewhere. But there are some which cannot be ignored. The continuance of the tragic conflict in Vietnam is a source of constant anxiety. We fervently hope that conditions will be created to enable the discussions to become more purposeful. The Vietnamese people must be assured of their inherent right to shape their destiny peacefully and without outside interference. We believe that the key to the next step still lies in the total cessation of the bombing of North Vietnam. In advocating this we are not actuated by a partisan spirit but by our sincere desire for peace and stability.

Another source of anxiety—the West Asian crisis—also needs to be resolved by political means. There is every opportunity for doing so, if it is recognized that the security, sovereignty and territorial integrity of the States in this part of the world cannot be based on the redrawing of State frontiers by force or on the basis of permanent hostility.

Essential for a peaceful settlement is the withdrawal of foreign forces from all Arab territories occupied in June last year. The process of the restoration of peace can begin and Ambassador Jarring's mission be fruitful only with the clear affirmation of this.

Equally explosive is the continued denial of basic human rights on grounds of race. The consciousness of the world community must be aroused not only against South Africa where racial discrimination has been elevated to the level of State policy, but against the emergence of racialism in any form in other areas. We must also firmly resist the last vestiges of colonialism. Our freedom and independence will not be complete so long as the people of South West Africa, Angola, Mozambique and Portuguese Guinea are denied theirs.

Recent events in Czechoslovakia have cast yet another shadow on the fragile structure for a new world order. The principles of non-interference by one State in the internal affairs of another, of scrupulous respect for the sovereignty, territorial integrity and political independence of all States are essential to the principle of peaceful co-existence. It is of the utmost importance that normal conditions should be restored without delay in Czechoslovakia.

If the use of force in international affairs is not renounced, and the rights of nations and the equality of races are not respected, how can tensions be reduced or the dangers of conflicts avoided? The world is caught in a vicious circle, because of which any viable international machinery to regulate relations between States is being progressively undermined and faces the danger of eventual collapse.

Nuclear weapons today represent the ultimate in force. Thus any attempt to eliminate force as the determining factor in international relations must begin with practical steps towards disarmament. But the nuclear menace has become an accepted fact of life and the world has developed a certain insensitivity to the nature of the threat. Despite every solemn resolution adopted by this Assembly, States continue to enlarge their capacity for nuclear war. The arms race and the search for more sophisticated weapons have rendered meaningless the concept of balance of power. Yet, every advance in military technology is accompanied by an effort to maintain a balance of terror. This encourages local wars and undermines the established political authority in States which are struggling to protect their freedom.

It is by restricting, reducing and eventually eliminating the growing nuclear menace that firm foundations of peace can be laid. The limited achievement of the partial test ban treaty has been off-set by the refusal of States to halt the testing of nuclear weapons. The problems of insecurity cannot be solved by imposing arbitrary restrictions on those who do not possess nuclear weapons, without any corresponding steps to deal with the basic problem of limiting stockpiles in the hands of a few Powers. How can the urge to acquire nuclear status be controlled so long as this imbalance persists? Unless the Powers which possess these weapons are prepared to exercise some self-restraint, collective efforts to rid the world of the nuclear menace cannot bear fruit.

We yearn for peace, not merely because it is good in itself, but because without peace there can be no improvement in the lives of the vast majority of the world's peoples. Development must receive the first priority and must be based on self-reliance. Our peoples expect their governments to build, in a generation, the apparatus of production and distribution which took the present advanced nations many centuries to install. Progress in technology and the acceleration of the processes of history will certainly help the developing nations to telescope the stages of their economic growth. But this acceleration works even more dramatically in favour of the affluent. The chasm between the rich and the poor nations, which is already a source of tension and bitterness in the world, is not decreasing but growing.

This situation is fraught with danger for the future well-being of our world. It is natural that we in the developing countries should be more aware of the peril than those who live in the affluent countries. The peril is on our doorstep, but it is not too far from theirs.

The world has changed, the membership of the United Nations has changed, but attitudes of mind have not. The representatives who are gathered here come from countries with distinct personalities. They have had great civilisations in the past—some known and some yet to be discovered. In the old colonial days, history, geography, culture and civilisation were all viewed from a particular perspective. Even today to be civilised is held to be synonymous with being westernised. Advanced countries devote large resources to formulating and spreading ideas and doctrines and they tend to impose on the developing nations their own norms and methods. The pattern of the classical acquisitive society with its deliberate multiplication of wants not only is unsuited to conditions in our countries but is positively harmful.

Developing nations have their special problems, and there is much scope for co-operation amongst themselves. Some problems are common, but the conditions in each country differ, and the same remedy cannot be prescribed for all. Those who seek to advise us seldom realise that we need new and different answers to our problems. We need solutions which are suited to our conditions, not imitative theories or techniques grafted from outside. We must make our own analysis of developments and how to deal with them. International forums such as this Assembly and the specialised agencies of the United Nations give us the opportunity to place our views before the world. But of what avail is this if we cannot forge the solidarity which would command attention?

Our problems are such as did not confront the advanced nations when they were at a similar stage of economic development. Freedom awakens hope. It generates consciousness of economic, social and political rights. As literacy spreads, as modern communications and close contacts grow with affluent countries, new expectations and tensions are created.

In India, our effort has been to build democracy and to develop a technologically mature society. Each in itself is a formidable endeavour in a country of our size. Demands grow much faster than the means to fulfil them, but changes do not come about easily. Every step forward meets with impediments created by the forces of the *status quo*. Every step forward, even though intended to end inequality, leads to a phase where inequality becomes more obvious or new inequalities come into existence. Let me give an example. We have introduced universal primary education and expanded higher education. We have done so because education is the key to the ending of existing disparities; because it is the greatest influence for modernisation and because it gives full scope to the flowering of the human personality. However, certain groups and regions which are already comparatively better off are able to take greater advantage of the new facilities: for example, the urban areas more than the rural, the rich farmers more than the poor peasants.

The affluence of the industrialised nations itself attracts and exerts a certain pull on the more fortunate sections in the developing countries, further sharpening the difference between aspirations and their fulfilment. This in turn leads to the alienation of the élite from the rest of society, because they are attracted by the glamour of catching up with their opposites in the advanced countries while their own society cries out for bread.

We are not unaware of the important developments taking shape within the affluent countries themselves, where increasing numbers have begun to question the purpose of their lives. Poverty and want must be eradicated, for they degrade the human personality. On the other hand, the affluent society, as it has emerged, seems to have become entangled in its instruments. Dazzled by its own glitter, it has lost sight of the goals it set out to achieve. It is natural, therefore, that societies which have stressed the importance of material possessions should anxiously seek a balance between spiritual and material values. This is still an intellectual groping which lacks articulation, but one can sense it in the restlessness of younger people and students, in the various forms of protest against traditional or established authority. There is a desire to assert individuality in technological societies which are becoming more uniform and more impersonal. Abundance without commitment to ideals will sow the seeds of discontent and invite its own disruption. Prosperity must be integrated with a higher purpose, and it should be the endeavour of all nations—it certainly is ours in India—to achieve harmony between progress and the timeless values of the spirit. We are human and do not always succeed; but, as Mahatma Gandhi said, "Satisfaction lies in the effort, not in the attainment."

The individual is no longer content to entrust to others the shaping of his destiny; he wants to be the master of his fate. So also with nations, which, while co-operating with others, wish to develop and progress according to their own genius and tradition. The question is vital for developing nations, which still have time to chart their course. The methods they use, the directions they take, will determine their goals.

We welcome any genuine form of international co-operation for the development of under-developed areas. At its best, foreign aid represents such an endeavour. But can it not also be legitimately described as a form of enlightened self-interest on the part of aid-giving countries, especially when it is tied with the purchase of equipment and of know-how from donor countries? In India, aid accounts for only a fifth of our total investment in development. Economic progress is not possible without investment. Not all the investment for Europe's progress came from the sweated labour of European workers and farmers. It came also from the peoples of Asia, Africa and South America who were denied a fair return for their work and their produce. Empires have ended, but the colonial pattern of economy remains with us in one form or another. As exporters of primary agricultural produce and minerals, we know to our cost how the terms of trade have steadily gone against us. Aid is only partial recompense for what their superior economic power of the advanced countries denies us through trade. Trade has the further advantage of placing greater responsibility on the developing nations, leading them towards self-reliance. I urge the nations assembled here to give their fullest support to the work initiated by the two United Nations Conferences on Trade and Development and to persuade the strong to dismantle the economic walls which they have built to defend themselves from the weak. In so doing they will be fortifying the defences of peace before it is too late.

These are the factors which cause tensions and bitterness, which divide society and lead it away from co-operation and the paths of peace.

Fear grips large parts of the world. Sages in my land exhorted us to be free from that which made us afraid, anticipating by thirty centuries those famous words of our own times, that there is nothing to fear but fear itself. No people were so cowed down as my countrymen before Mahatma Gandhi came on the scene. India was able to wrest freedom because he taught us to overcome fear and hatred and to be absorbed in a cause which was greater than ourselves.

We in India are attuned to the idea that the paths to truth are many and various. An attempt to remake the world in any one image will not be countenanced by the majority of mankind. Our age has been called the space age, but I would call it the age of the people. Revolutionaries, liberators and political leaders have always talked of the people, but for the first time now, "we the people" does not mean a few representing the many, but the masses themselves, each of whom is poignantly conscious of his individuality, each one of whom is seeking to assert his rights and to voice his demands.

Through the ages, man has struggled against vastly superior forces. The one constant has been his indomitable spirit. He has pitted his puny frame against nature. He has fought against tremendous odds for freedom, for his beliefs, for an idea or an ideal. Endowed with such a spirit, will man abdicate in favour of the machine or bow to the dominance of tyranny in new garbs? Men have been tortured, men have been killed, but the idea has prevailed.

Two years hence, in 1970, the United Nations will complete twenty-five years. Can we make it a Year of Peace—a starting point of a united endeavour to give mankind the blessings of a durable peace? To this end let us devote ourselves. One of our ancient prayers says:

Common be your prayer;	Common be your desire;
Common be your end;	Unified be your hearts;
Common be your purpose;	Unified be your intentions;
Common be your deliberation.	Perfect be the union among you.

3. FOREIGN POLICY DETERMINANTS, 1970*

Foreign policy cannot be divorced from a country's internal policy.

*Address at a seminar on "Some Aspects of Our Foreign Policy" organised by the Congress Party in Parliament and the A.I.C.C. at Mavalankar Hall, August 31, 1970.

Any country, any Government, any political party must decide what it believes in, and all its policies must then flow from this basic conviction or belief. What is our foreign policy? Some people take the word "non-alignment" and think that is the whole of our foreign policy. In a way it is not the word "non-alignment", but what non-alignment stands for, namely that we believe in independently judging all issues. We do not wish to be tied to any group or to any country.

We are today nearer to the twenty-first century than we are to the nine-teenth. But unfortunately we find that over large portions of the world, thinking is still very much as in the nineteenth century. The world has changed; we helped to change it because of India's freedom movement, because of India becoming free, and other countries in Asia and Europe becoming free. This has been the greatest change in the world. Although it was obvious to us that we would become free and that our freedom would lead to the freedom of other countries, this process came somewhat as a shock to the colonial powers.

For some time they seemed to be stunned by that shock, but it has not taken long for them to recover. And since they have recovered, we see another very subtle change coming over the world, rather dangerous change, which is that colonialism—open, frank, honest colonialism—has given way to a veiled neo-colonialism. This has actually happened in some places and in other places there have been attempts that it should happen.

Therefore the difficulties before the developing countries are still very great. And we can face them not merely by idealism, not merely by sentimentalism, but by very clear thinking and hard-headed analysis.

There are those who say that non-alignment has not served our purpose or that it has not been a success. What is the alternative? Obviously, that we should be aligned. If we should be aligned, then with whom should we be aligned? The two major blocs are what are commonly known as Eastern and Western blocs. Should we be aligned with the Eastern bloc? Before we go on to alignment, we must recognise that alignment has had many cracks in the last few years in both the blocs. Should we join any of these cracked blocs?

I am sure anybody who looks clearly at this picture will immediately come to the conclusion that it would not be in our interest to join any blocs. Therefore, we come back to the third position, which is outside of the blocs. I do not think it is an idealistic position. I think it is the only hard-headed, practical path that is open to any country which wants to keep itself independent.

Many of those who have been against non-alignment all these years and who criticised my father and myself for trying to pursue this path are today not attacking non-alignment as such, but are saying that we are not truly non-aligned. The great attack today, the greatest weapon which is used against foreign policy, is to say that in effect we are following the Soviet line. Perhaps they think their saying so will frighten us into trying to give up our friendship with the Soviet Union. Perhaps they merely think that they will be able to blow up the image of independence which we have amongst our own people and in the world. Let us be very clear that, regardless of what our big newspapers say here, the image of India is very clear outside. It is not an image of a country which follows any group or country; it is an image of a country standing or trying to stand squarely on its own feet. It does not mean that they always think we are right. Many of the countries think that we make mistakes. And on many occasions we go wrong. On all the occasions when we seem to support the Western countries, it is the Eastern group which says we have gone wrong or we have not been strong enough. On those occasions when we have supported the Soviet Union, or more likely the African-Asian countries, the Western world thinks we have gone wrong.

On one occasion, the American Ambassador complained to me that we had supported the Soviet Union on more occasions in the United Nations than we had supported other countries. I said: "Let us look at each occasion." I did not have details with me there and then, because this remark was made at a party. But I said: "If you look at the occasions on which we have seemed to side with the Soviet Union, what do you find? Were they not issues in which India and the developing countries were vitally interested? And if this was so, would it not be more true to say that the Soviet Union had supported the stand taken by the developing countries, by the African and Asian countries, and not that we had gone out of our way to support the Soviet Union?" Afterwards I put this question to the Ministry of External Affairs and actually when we counted up, we found that it was not even true to say that we had voted with the Soviet Union on more occasions than we had voted with the other countries. Even the basic point which the Ambassador had made did not turn out to be correct.

So the tendency to make sweeping generalisations is very greatly prevalent, perhaps everywhere. We can only see the situation in our country. And the tendency to see a subject or a particular issue super-ficially without studying the background is also rather prevalent among the oppressed and other sections of the people here. Therefore it is import-ant to go into each subject in some depth.

Basically, what do we want from our foreign policy? What is the ideal we pursue? Is that ideal divorced from the practical interest of the country, or is it allied with it? As it happens, our ideal and practical interests are the same. No Government can afford, however idealistic it may be, to leave or neglect the practical interests of the country. We have believed—and we do believe now—that freedom is indivisible, that peace is indivisi-ble, that economic prosperity is indivisible. And these are the fundament-als on which our foreign policy is based, both inside the country and outside. We have stood for the freedom of all countries. Even when we were not free, when we were in no position to help other countries, we went out of our way to give them whatever moral and other support we could. And I know that that moral support was welcomed and it did help these countries. Today we have the same stand. We know that joining together with the Afro-Asian group is not immediately going to strengthen any of the countries who belong to that group. But we know that there is no other way of strengthening them either. We share the common problems, common difficulties, common threats. And we can face them only by trying to stand on our own feet, by having stability within our country and by having economic progress. We think we can have stabil-ity and progress only if we take a particular economic path—the path of socialism through which we give social justice to our people. It is the same social justice in the international sphere for which we stand. We believe that while there are poor nations and rich nations, there is bound to be tension.

There is not only tension between the poor and the rich, but there is tension among the rich because of their desire to control or to influence the developing nations. This is how in the past most wars took place and this is the reason for much of the tension today. Yet you find that in spite of the tension, again and again countries try to follow the path which we have advocated, namely the path of conciliation and of trying to solve problems by means of negotiation rather than by war.

In my Independence Day speech I spoke about two recent events. No two countries could have fought more bitterly than the Soviet Union and Germany. There have been many wars, but I do not think one has seen such great bitterness in any as in the war which took place between these two countries, because the fighting was not merely nation to nation, it was not merely province to province, in Stalingrad it was a house-to-house fighting which was almost a fight for each brick of the city of Stalingrad. Perhaps you still remember that while men were fighting, the women were picking up the bricks to show that Stalingrad could stand and fight the war. So you can understand what tremendous feeling and personal involvement there was among the people. And yet, today these two countries have been able to have an agreement to try and solve their difficulties or problems through talking about them openly, forgetting that bitterness, that hatred, which was not a hatred of a few years, but a hatred that went a long way into history. Yet they made this agreement. Nobody knows whether the talks will succeed—it does not matter whether they will succeed. Naturally we would like them to succeed. But even if they do not succeed, a very important step has been taken, a step which, according to our policy, we have been trying in our country and in other countries. Similarly, there has been an acceptance of the method of negotiation in what we call Western Asia and what in the Western world is called the Middle East.

Now foreign policy has to be based on one's historical and geographical background. That is, we see the world from where we are. Other countries see the world from where they are. So we cannot possibly see it from exactly the same angle. We have certain countries for our neighbours. So it is important what relationship we have with our neighbouring countries. If we are a long way from other countries, we can look at them from different angles.

We also find that in the making of the foreign policy of any country, and perhaps specially of India, there are certain intangible elements which are just as important or decisive in forming our point of view. It is perhaps easier to pursue foreign policy and fashion our relations with other countries if one is a rich and a powerful nation. Now India is not a rich or a powerful nation, and we have to keep that in view. Nevertheless we have made up for our lack of riches and power with some other qualities which we possess.

Earlier, because we were in the forefront of the freedom struggle, that gave us a certain influence. Also because we had leaders of stature who were able to give inspiration to other countries who were in similar position as we were. Today that situation has changed. All these countries have been free for a number of years; they are all trying to stand on their own feet and none of them would like to be guided by any other country. They would like to have friends, but they would not like to feel that any one country is superior to them. We ourselves perhaps would not like that position. So we can understand that other countries, and especially countries which are smaller, do not like that position, and we should be very careful that at no time we give an impression that we are wanting to take a leading position. That would immediately mean that we are trying to push them towards a somewhat backward position.

So when we find ourselves in the situation which we are in, that is, in an extremely difficult economic and political situation where you do not have power, then either you have to stand firm on your convictions and try to strengthen yourself, or you strengthen yourself through alliances. As I said earlier, there are people in our country who think that we could ally ourselves with some people and perhaps that way we would be safer. I do not think that such borrowed strength can be real strength, and I think the feeling of security which one would get could be rather deceiving. It would not be real security, and it would deceive us into a feeling of complacency and really lead us into certain dangerous situations later on. I think the only security is to strengthen our own people and to be confident of ourselves.

I mentioned earlier the intangible elements. These are conviction, courage and national pride. And I would not like anybody to think that the pride which I have in view is the very chauvinistic, narrow-minded pride which is put forward sometimes by some parties in our country who think that national pride consists of getting offended or feeling insulted at the slightest thing that happens. It is only a weak nation lacking self-confidence which feels insulted by other people. As I have said in the House, nobody can be degraded except by his own actions; no country can be degraded except by the country's own behaviour and action. And being poor or weak in the way we are poor and weak is not degrading. It is not a good thing and we must change that state of affairs. But by itself it is not a degrading thing. If because of our poverty and our economic condition and our lack of military or other strength, we were to allow ourselves to give up what is in the national interest, that would be degrading.

And what are we doing? We are trying to strengthen ourselves. We have strengthened ourselves, perhaps slowly, but step by step over the years we have strengthened ourselves not only in the military sense but also in the economic sense. Further, we have stood by what we believe in, regardless of its consequence, in all the forums of the world and that is why we are today respected. Nobody is going to think ill of us because we come to an understanding with some smaller countries if we have some difference of opinion with them. On the contrary, people will blame us for trying to throw our weight about, or trying to pressurise small countries if we have any differences with them. Of course, in all such matters national interests and national honour must come first, but we must not confuse this with any narrow chauvinistic attitude.

I think it was some British statesman who said that no country is a permanent foe or a permanent friend. Any country must try to be friends with as many countries as possible. As I have said in the A.I.C.C., all our policy is to strengthen existing friendships, to change indifference into friendship, and to lessen the hostility where it exists. Sometimes the assertion is made that India has no friends. This is the most peculiar statement which I have heard. I would like to say that if we are counting friends, which country has got friends? I have heard from practically every power—and I include in this some of the very big super-powers—the same complaint that they have no friends. It just depends on how you count. What is the measuring tape for friendship? It is possible that one of the senses in which people have understood friendship is how many countries will come and help us when we have a war. How many countries, whom we call friends, would really be able to help? The fact is that India today has about as many friends as any other country has. How we keep those friends or whether they remain friends is not dependent merely on what we do, but what happens to be their national interests at any given time. If it is in their interests to be friends with us, they will be friends and if it is not in their national interests, it does not matter what we do, they still will not be our friends. So, we must try to increase our friendship, but all the time we have to be prepared for any other situation when the same country may not be a friend or a country which is not our friend may decide for various reasons to become our friend. Our whole attitude must be flexible in all these matters.

It does not help us at any time to merely speak ill of a country. If we want to do something against a country now, let us make up our minds and take some steps. But while we are not taking such steps, or do not consider such steps desirable, it does not serve any useful purpose merely to shout about that country. Even the biggest of the super-powers has found that war should be avoided. They have proceeded in such a manner that they have got into trouble and all their armies, all their power, all their influence, has not been able to help them to get out of the mess. The basic conviction and belief in certain ideas cannot change. That is a constant whether it is in domestic policy or whether it is in foreign policy.

As I said earlier, courage and conviction must be allied to an astute, hard-headed analysis of international affairs and events. At all times this analysis has to be devoid of emotion and sentiment. We have found that the very growth of military power in the hands of a few countries is producing its own antithesis. There are nations with military stockpiles of unimaginable destructive potential who are today unable to use that power. One gun-boat could do much more in olden times than what very much greater arsenals are able to do today, because of the fear of the consequences of using them.

We are friends today with the United States and the USSR as well as with a lot of other countries. We are helped by many of these countries and we have tried not to be dependent on any one of these countries. We have tried to diversify even the buying of essentials from different countries and at the same time to try and become self-sufficient and to stand on our own feet. But in today's world no country can be absolutely independent of another. It is a world of interdependence. But you can be interdependent only if you are secure in your freedom. If you give up part of your freedom, that relationship changes; then it is not interdependence; it becomes something else; it becomes a form of—well I won't say slavery, but some form of colonialism comes in. In the life of a city or anywhere else in earlier days, each person or each group was very much more self-sufficient. They produced everything they needed. They were content with what they could produce. Each community became a complete sort of unit. Today it is not so. Each city is dependent on some other cities; each State is dependent on other States to a certain extent. This is the situation in the world at large. We may get some of our necessary things from the developed countries but the developed countries can also not exist without a great deal of things from the other countries. We have to see that the relationship is such that it cannot force us into any position which is not in our interest. This is where we have to be firm, and that is why we want to be self-reliant in all the essentials so that at no time can anybody say: Well, you need this, you cannot get it until you do such and such thing. This is the position which we have avoided and which we will continue to avoid.

As I said, although we get many essential things from other countries at no time has this forced us to change our policy in any manner at all. We have stuck to whatever we believe in and the world has respected us for it. So when the United States or the Soviet Union helps us through financial credits, which are wrongly termed as "aid", or by enabling us to produce industrial and defence equipment, we presume that they do it out of their own national self-interest. But our own national interests compel us to build up our economic and defence strength with the help of whoever is prepared to give it and help us to stand on our own feet. Therefore, we will not allow ourselves to be led away either by the anti-Soviet hysteria or by anti-America hysteria.

As you know, I am going to Lusaka next week to attend the Conference of Non-aligned and the question has frequently been asked in the last few weeks: "What good will this Conference be and what do we hope to get out of it?" I personally think that the very fact of meeting a large number of Heads of State and sharing experiences with them is a very useful event. While we try to keep in touch with people through letters and through our Embassies, this does not and cannot take the place of personal contact and personal discussions not only in the forum of the Conference, but individually and informally. So this by itself would be a very important reason for holding such a conference.

It is amazing to see that when the non-aligned Asian and African nations get together, some newspapers find all kinds of words such as "jamboree" and "picnic", but when other nations get together, then those words are never used. They say they have a serious meeting or a common problem. We do not have common problems, of course. I think it is just amazing, and what is more amazing is that even when all predictions turn out wrong, there is no hesitation to go in the same path and make the same predictions again. But nobody now is taken in by this kind of comment or this kind of reaction. We know that many of the allied countries do not like this non-aligned group to exist, whether they are on one side or the other. Neither of them like it. Most of these super-powers would like to have spheres of influence. Although we are very friendly with them, we do not agree with this attitude of theirs and we are certainly not going to help them to have this kind of sphere of influence. The only sphere of influence we want is one of friendship and of mutual help, and I think that in the kind of conference of non-aligned, which is being held in Lusaka, there can be mutual help especially in the economic sphere. It is not easy because, although many of the problems are the same, conditions are different and there are many pressures on all of these countries. But if we are able to help one another even to understand the pressures to a small extent, I think this Conference will have served a useful purpose. So we meet together to reinforce our economic and political independence and to tell the world that we want to throw our weight in favour of peace. We do not want a balance of power in favour of power, but in favour of peace.

I do not want to go here into the specifics of our dealings with various nations, as Mr. Sharma told us that this was done by Sardar Swaran Singh and the other people who have spoken here before me. But I would like to say that I think that it is possible through friendship to outmanoeuvre hostility. And this, indeed, if you read Indian history, is the sum total of our tradition from the days of the Buddha and the Emperor Ashoka right down to our own times of Mahatma Gandhi and Jawaharlal Nehru. These great personages have showed us the essence of our tradition and Gandhiji specially brought it out from the safe-keeping of an ideal into the very business of daily living, the hurly-burly of political and economic policy. I think it would be a very great mistake to give this up for what may be considered to be a temporary gain as some of our friends of the Right and sometimes our friends of the Left keep advising us to do. Our Party is the central force in Indian life. We have the responsibility whereas those who are not in power have the freedom and the right to advocate courses which may not necessarily be responsible.

We have seen that our people have risen and have stood and worked as one man in every crisis which the nation has faced and it is this knowledge that we in India shall defend our freedom, if need be with our bare fists, that has acted as a deterrent to those who may have other thoughts about us. But if we permit this will and determination to be weakened and softened by internal conflict, then no amount of arms will help us. Arms used by people without conviction cannot provide any credible backing for foreign policy. Therefore, while we must have arms to defend our country from any aggression, these arms, this military strength must be backed by conviction in our ideals and confidence in ourselves. Both are equally great weapons and without them the other weapons can be dangerous to ourselves and can also be impotent in helping to defend ourselves. This is the essence of our foreign policy. And if we understand this essence and keep it, we have a certain amount of man-oeuvrability. Why do Governments of India not wish to make categorical statements sometimes? Because it is not in our interest to be known as being stuck in any given position. When we are rigid, it helps those who are against us. They will have manoeuvrability and can move about, while we are stuck. We become a good target for anybody.

Therefore, we must have a certain amount of flexibility and manoeuvra-bility, but, as I said, it must be consistent with national interest and honour and we cannot manoeuvre or change where basic convictions and basic ideals, aims and objectives are concerned. If we keep this in view, then I think India will not only keep its position but will be able to enhance it in the world. I certainly hope that all of you who are present here, or all other members of our great Party, will be able to give this knowledge and understanding to our country and to our people. It is not enough to reach the educated whom we can reach through seminars, but you must go to the villages and the rural areas to explain these matters to rural people, tell them how closely foreign policy is connected with domestic policy, how closely what happens in far-away countries affects things that happen in our country. It is only then that we will be able to have that united force which can make our country great.

Once again I thank you for giving me this opportunity of placing some of my thoughts before you. I congratulate you on this very good idea and on the excellent manner in which I am told you have been able to translate it into action.

4. NON-ALIGNED COUNTRIES CONFERENCE, LUSAKA, 1970*

Here in Lusaka we can feel the ebb and flow of the continuing battle against remnants of colonialism in Angola and Mozambique. We can

*Address at the Third Conference of Non-Aligned Countries held at Lusaka, September 9, 1970.

feel the vibrations of the struggle against the minority Government in Zimbabwe, and the apartheid policies of the racist regime in the Union of South Africa, and of the stirrings of the national movements in Namibia and in Guinea Bissau. These freedom fighters are engaged in the same battle as we were only recently. They are risking their lives for the same principles that we hold dear. We extend our support to these brave men and women.

As I said yesterday, the revolution of our times is unfinished, and the purpose of the Conference is to draw up a clear programme of action to carry it forward. This is the challenge that the decade of the Seventies places before the non-aligned countries.

Only a short while ago, the issues of war and peace, of the disposal of human beings and their destinies, were decided in a few capitals of the world. No longer is it so; because millions of people in the resurgent continents of Asia, of Africa, of Latin America and the Caribbeans, have come into their own; because we determined that decisions involving us, whether concerning war and peace, or the direction and pace of our social, economic and political development, could be made only by us, in our own way, and in our own countries. That is how non-alignment was born. It expressed our individual and collective sovereignty, our devotion to freedom and peace, and our urgent need to give to our people a better life and the opportunity to live in freedom, in dignity and in peace. At no time was there any intention to set up a third world.

This is our endeavour. The odds are tremendous. Each step has met with criticism and opposition. But we have carried on. Let us not be deterred by cynics and the hostile propaganda of the powerful media of communications. From the beginning, there has been no lack of inquisitors, who looked upon non-alignment as heresy and distorted its meaning. They said it would not work. But we can answer back in the famous words of Galileo: "And yet—it moves"!

The criticism of non-alignment has shifted on two counts. Those who now concede that non-alignment had some utility in the days of the cold war confrontation, maintain that this is no longer so. The reviling is not any more about the basis and principle, but of its practice.

Have the non-aligned States lost their relevance? The answer is an emphatic no. Twenty-five years after the last holocaust, the world is not yet on the brink of peace. The nuclear balance of terror still confronts us. The war in Vietnam is said to be waged with "conventional" weapons, yet these include chemical contamination of food and plant life. The only way to have a clean war is not to have a war at all. Hence India stands and works for total disarmament.

The great powers certainly have the major responsibility for international peace and security. We welcome all initiatives towards the resolution of differences through negotiations, but even if they reach accord on their common interests, and decide upon mutually acceptable limitation of strategic arsenals, the rest of the world, of which we form a considerable part, could hardly remain mere onlookers. We have an equal stake in peace, but the quality of this peace should be such as will ensure our own sovereignty and security.

Not only national honour but national interest demands that we do not mortgage our decisions in domestic and in international affairs to foreign dictate. This was one element of our policy of non-alignment. As the logical corollary, we rejected the enmities of our erstwhile rulers. As my father declared: "We are in no camp and in no military alliance. The only camp we should like to be in is the camp of peace which should include as many countries as possible." May I thank the Conference for its gracious gesture in memory of my father and the many distinguished delegates for their kind references to him?

We decided that our respective territories should not be used for the subjugation of other people, for subversion, or for the carving out of spheres of influence. Indian manpower and resources had been used for imperialist purposes. Once free, we declared that this would no longer be permitted.

We have all been subjected to domination, exploitation and the humiliation of racial discrimination. How could we compromise with racialism in any form? The pernicious theory that one man is superior to another merely on the ground of race or birth has been proved to be false, yet it continues to dominate the thinking of many.

Today's world is a single entity. We are deeply convinced that by staying out of military pacts, the non-aligned countries can use their collective wisdom and influence to tip the balance of power in favour of peace and international co-operation.

These have been the positive achievements of non-alignment. If today belief in the efficacy of military pacts has weakened, if historic animosities are giving way to essays in friendship and co-operation, if a breath of realism is influencing international policies towards *detente*, the nations assembled here can claim some credit. However, this should not lull us into complacency.

The big powers have never accepted the validity of non-alignment. Neither colonialism nor racialism has vanished. The old comes back in new guise. There are subtle intrigues to undermine our self-confidence and to sow dissension and mutual distrust amongst us. Powerful vested interests, domestic and foreign, are combining to erect new structures of neo-colonialism. These dangers can be combated by our being united in our adherence to the basic tenets of non-alignment.

I have touched upon certain general points, but, on such an occasion, one cannot ignore some of the explosive situations which confront the world.

I should like to take this opportunity to convey our admiration and best wishes to President Nasser for his statesmanship and courage in accepting the cease-fire. We disapprove of Israel's intransigence. Israel should be prevailed upon to comply fully with the UN Security Council Resolution of November, 1967. We cannot deny to the people of Palestine their inalienable right to the homelands from which they were exiled.

The situation in South-East Asia has further deteriorated. We are deeply concerned about the spreading of the conflict to Cambodia. All foreign forces should withdraw from the various countries of Indo-China, the lead being given by the U.S.A. Our assessment, based on talks with the various parties concerned, has led us to believe that a broad-based government comprising all elements of South Vietnam would pave the way for the success of the Paris talks. Recent developments in Laos indicate the possibility of talks between the two sides there. As Member and Chairman of the International Commission, we have offered our good offices to both the concerned parties for this purpose. To preserve peace and to provide for the reconstruction of this war-torn area, some kind of international convention or agreement should be signed by all the parties concerned as well as the great powers and other interested parties to ensure respect for the neutrality, independence, territorial integrity and sovereignty of all the Indo-China States.

We have been deeply disturbed by the reported intention of the United Kingdom and other Governments to supply arms to the Government of South Africa. This dangerous and retrograde step will threaten the neighbours of South Africa and also the Indian Ocean area. Any accretion to South Africa's military capability will abet its policy of apartheid and racial discrimination, and may encourage it to annex other territories. The argument that this is being done to protect the so-called security of sea routes is untenable. We would like the Indian Ocean to be an area of peace and co-operation. Foreign military bases will create tension and great-power rivalry.

The spirit of freedom goes hand in hand with the spirit of equality. Beyond the political problems of the Unfinished Revolution, there are complex and difficult economic tasks. However, a realistic appraisal of our natural resources, our capacities and our competence reveals the possibility of our working together to reduce our dependence on those who do not respect our sovereignty so that economic leverage for thinly disguised political purposes cannot be used against us. Neo-colonialism has no sympathy with our efforts to achieve self-reliance. It seeks to perpetuate our position of disadvantage. International markets are so manipulated that primary producing countries have a permanent handicap. The levers of technology also are operated against us through unequal collaboration and royalty agreements.

Hence we have to redouble our effort to gain for each nation the opportunity to develop to its full stature. The primary responsibility rests upon each developing country, but we also owe a duty to one another. The fallacy that there is no complementality between our economies has so far made it difficult to realise the undoubted potential of mutual co-operation. There is greater complementality amongst our economies than between the economies of developed nations. Yet, advanced nations have been more successful in forging instruments of co-operation amongst themselves and our own effort in this direction has not even begun. The potential of trade and economic co-operation amongst us has been left virtually unexplored. By meeting each other's needs, we would diversify our trade, safeguard it against the caprices of international commerce, and reduce our dependence on middlemen and brokers.

This Conference should formulate the manner in which we could strengthen one another, and give due priority in our national policies to positive measures for mutual co-operation. Such co-operation will help each of us to find some solutions to our respective problems, and also give us the capability to induce these changes in the economic system at the global level.

Through the United Nations Conference on Trade and Development, we have tried to persuade the international community to make changes which have been overdue in the economic system. This is now well understood all over the world. But only some have been accepted in principle, and even their implementation has been tardy. In a few weeks, the Second Development Decade will be launched by the UN General Assembly. So far, there has been little progress in evolving guidelines for international co-operation. Many nations which have the capacity, and if I may say so the duty, to make a decisive contribution, hedge their statements with reservations. For too long has international co-operation been viewed as a one-way traffic from the rich to the poor nations.

As the Prime Minister of Guyana said yesterday, between ourselves we possess the major part of the world's natural resources. Our manpower resources are no less plentiful. It should not be beyond our ingenuity to develop these resources, and employ the manpower for the production of wealth for our peoples. Because of historical circumstances, economic relations have not been developed as among ourselves, but between each of our countries and the erstwhile metropolitan powers. We can now make the first attempts to discover areas of co-operation in many fields of development—generation of power, development of agriculture, improvement of roadways, railways and telecommunications, the expansion of higher education and training in science and technology. If we decide—and I hope we shall—to make a beginning with this study, India will be glad to play her modest part.

We all recognise the malaise afflicting the development process. We know of the growing gap between developed and developing countries, between the northern and southern hemispheres, of the indifference of the affluent, the disappointments of the First Development Decade, and the failure of the affluent countries to transfer even one per cent of their gross national product. We are painfully familiar with the pitfalls of "aid", in which the bulk of credits are tied to purchases from donor countries, and with the fact that a big portion of new credits goes to the repayment of old loans. But the question is: Must we endlessly wait in the hope that some day the developed countries will undergo a change of heart and acknowledge that disparities in the world are not in their own interest? It would be unrealistic to expect miracles of magnanimity. Even if this should happen, I am afraid that it would be of no avail, in the absence of the right conditions in our own countries. We must determine to help ourselves, to sacrifice, to pool our resources of knowledge and initiative. We must work together on a bilateral, regional and multilateral basis.

From my own experience, I have learnt that will-power, unceasing endeavour and the capacity for sacrifice sustained and strengthened us during struggle for political independence. These same qualities will help us towards economic freedom.

The power to question is the basis of all human progress. We are free because we questioned the right of others to rule over us. But intellectual and cultural emancipation is just beginning. We are rediscovering ourselves, and the fact that a country sees things in terms of its own geography and history. Those who dominated the world's political affairs, and manned its economic controls, also imposed a monopoly of ideas. For years we accepted their values, their image of the world and, strangely enough, even of ourselves. Whether we like it or not, we have been pushed into postures of imitation. We have now to break away from borrowed models of development and evolve models of the worth-while life which are more relevant to our own conditions—not necessarily as a group but as individual countries with distinctive personalities.

The world today is united in peril, not merely the peril from nuclear destruction but the more insidious daily pollution of our environment. We should be united in prosperity, and in the blossoming of the spirit of man. The non-aligned countries must be in the vanguard of the movement to create the world of tomorrow and to enrich the content of human life.

The Unfinished Revolution can reach fulfilment if we have faith and confidence in ourselves and the assurance that, however long and arduous the journey ahead, we shall reach our destination.

5. UN GENERAL ASSEMBLY, 1970*

This jubilee celebration is tinged with anxiety and the mood is one of self-examination. The United Nations was born out of the experience of the Second World War, and out of a desire "to save succeeding generations from the scourge of war", and to promote universal respect for fundamental human rights and international justice. Its founders were conscious of the attempt of a previous generation to build the League of Nations, and of the reasons for its collapse.

Franklin D. Roosevelt declared that the United Nations spelt "the end of the system of unilateral action and exclusive alliance, and spheres of influence, and balance of power and all the other expedients which have been used for centuries and which have failed". "We propose," he went on

*Address to the United Nations General Assembly, October 23, 1970.

to say, "to substitute for these a universal organisation which all peace-loving nations will have a chance to join."

Twenty-five years later, the principle of the universality of the United Nations membership does not yet prevail. The system of unilateral action and exclusive alliances has not been disowned. Spheres of influence and balance of power continue to actuate the policies of many nations, even though they fail to produce the desired results.

Thus the United Nations has been afflicted by the same malady as the League of Nations, that is, the attempt to direct and control its activities and to use it as an instrument for national ends. To the extent it could be so used it was applauded, and when it did not serve such purpose it was ignored.

The right of a people to choose their form of government is in name only. In reality, there is considerable interference in the internal affairs of many countries. The powerful make their presence felt in many ways, relentlessly attempting to enlarge their spheres of influence. The extension of their military commitments to new areas inevitably attracts counter-action by other powers. The limited wars which we have witnessed in the last twenty-five years are the consequence of such policies.

Two such conflicts have dragged on for years, in the Middle East and in Vietnam. Our views have been reiterated here a few days ago. In the Middle East the relevant question is whether, in our age, we can allow the frontiers of States to be changed by force of arms. We feel that territories occupied by force must be vacated. That is why we support the Security Council Resolution of November 1967. Peace and security can come only with neighbourliness and understanding.

Recently one set of proposals was made by President Nixon on Vietnam, and another by the Provisional Revolutionary Government. Some common ground must be found between the two proposals. We hope that they are not regarded as final by either side. Perhaps an agreement on the complete withdrawal of all foreign forces, beginning with American forces, can lead to purposeful negotiations.

The United Nations has not been able to prevent these wars or bring about a settlement. But it has been the peacemaker in several conflicts. It has provided a useful mediating agency and meeting place where arrangements have been hammered out. Even those who feel that the United Nations has not fulfilled its original hopes do recognise that the world needs an international organisation which will work for peace and the peaceful resolution of conflicts. If the United Nations were to disintegrate, would we not find it necessary to establish some other international organisation for the same objectives? Let us therefore preserve what we have, breathe new meaning and purpose into it, so that it can create an order where the use of force would defeat its own purpose.

Countries which, like us, have won freedom newly, have attachment for this organisation and a special stake in its functioning. We are aware that old attitudes persist; at the same time there is some difference, however small. Recent events have shown that military power alone does not give full control of the situation on all occasions because other national wills, even of smaller nations, are also at work.

I have come here to reiterate my country's deep commitment to the principles and purposes of the Charter. Ever since India became sovereign, the United Nations has occupied a pivotal position in her foreign policy. In his very first policy statement after India attained freedom, Jawaharlal Nehru declared:

> The world, in spite of its rivalries and hatred and inner conflicts, moves inevitably towards closer co-operation and the building up of a world commonwealth. It is for this One World that free India will work, a world in which there is the free co-operation of free peoples, and no class or group exploits another.

All these twenty-five years, we have striven to make the United Nations stronger, and to defend it from the corrosive effects of cynicism. We have borne burdens on its behalf, undertaking missions of peace to Korea, the Gaza strip, and Congo. We have endeavoured to serve the cause of peace in Indo-China. We have sought to reconcile conflicting viewpoints in this forum. And we have resisted attempts to subordinate the United Nations to powerful national wills.

The recent Lusaka Conference of non-aligned countries, in which nearly half the members of the United Nations participated, reaffirmed the faith of non-aligned countries in this world organisation and resolved to work to strengthen it. We may not have technological power or nuclear arsenals, but our voice has to be heard. The United Nations should take full advantage of the support of these governments, and also of the inmost desire for peace which exists in the peoples of all nations. That is what enabled the United Nations to survive the cold war. Its influence can be enhanced by keeping it above power politics.

The great revolutionary cycle which was set in motion by the struggles for independence, by the yearning for equality, by the search for a new meaning in life, is not yet complete. In Lusaka, we pledged ourselves to complete the Unfinished Revolution of our times. Rekindling faith in itself, the United Nations must concern itself with this unfinished task. Vast political changes have taken place, but some countries still find themselves under the yoke of colonialism. The world organisation must work for their liberation. Where theories of racial superiority determine governmental policies, the United Nations must work for racial equality. We cannot view with equanimity the supply of arms to South Africa. The total abolition of colonialism and racialism in every form is a prerequisite of a new world order.

Political freedom is incomplete if it does not lead to wider horizons of economic opportunity, and this is possible only with peace. Hence, apart from preventing suffering and dispelling fear and uncertainty, disarmament would make a decisive difference to development. India has always used such influence as she had to achieve the acceptance of total disarmament. Nearly twenty years ago, we were instrumental in bringing about a private meeting of the great powers which ultimately led to the Test Ban Treaty. However, the Nuclear Non-Proliferation Treaty, which was formulated later, does not stop the production of nuclear weapons or remove stockpiles, but perpetuates the division between nuclear powers and others, thus creating yet another vested interest.

The world has become accustomed to nuclear arsenals, and insensitive to their evil, perhaps even unable to comprehend the sheer magnitude of the fearsome destruction they hold. There is a helpless acceptance of nuclear, biological and chemical weapons as part of our daily lives. Our preoccupation with smaller day-to-day problems clouds a careful examation of the assumptions and policies which have led to the arms race.

Ironically enough, neither those who possess the stockpiles, nor those who seek to be protected, feel secure. Power undermines itself from within and turns into impotence. As the Buddha said, "Iron turns to rust and rust devours iron."

Even a small reduction in the production of armaments would release vast material and technological resources for human welfare and would help the narrowing of economic disparities.

So far as we the independent developing nations are concerned, economic development has only just begun. We have our failings. We allowed our growth to be inhibited by structural and other difficulties—an outmoded social system and attitudes of mind, an administrative machine which was devised by foreign rulers for their own purposes. Many other difficulties are inherent in under-development. But our biggest impediment has been the attitudes of the strong nations, the kind of terms which they have set for financial outflows to the developing countries and the manner in which the poor nations are shut out from their markets. It will be difficult for our endeavour to succeed so long as technological neo-colonialism persists.

Tomorrow at our Commemorative Session when the Second Development Decade will be proclaimed, we shall formally adopt the international development strategy which has already been endorsed by the General Assembly and which moves forward from the archaic donor-donee relationship between developed and developing countries to the concept of partnership. Full support to measures outlined in the strategy by all member States of the United Nations can make a material contribution to the objectives enshrined in the Charter and revive faith in international economic co-operation. However, whether the strategy succeeds or not, the developing countries should not remain passive spectators. It is imperative for us to intensify our own efforts vigorously to the maximum extent possible in our countries and to develop trade and economic co-operation with one another. We can be effective if we are united. We must plan further than one decade. In the coming twenty-five years we should evolve a concept of a larger freedom for man.

Let it not be thought that I consider the affluent powers alone at fault. We are no more virtuous than they—only our weakness makes it appear so. Sometimes our own attitudes and conditions encourage their moves. I am acutely conscious that we ourselves have been content unimaginatively to follow the beaten track and have offered no alternative vision. Even movements which questioned the concept of an acquisitive society have, in the course of time, drifted into the same patterns.

International organisations tend to use as a basis for discussion and decision certain yardsticks of progress in economic functioning and so on, which have been evolved in a few countries in circumstances entirely different from those in the developing countries. Some nations use men, money and propaganda to impose their economic philosophy on others. The United Nations and its Agencies should not accept such premises automatically and elevate them to universal dogmas. Each problem must be viewed in its own setting. No nation should be uprooted from its special heritage, and the programmes for its progress must grow out of its own experience. In India we should like to build a distinctive design of life by re-examining the sources of our history, and by separating the perennial from the transitory in our tradition.

Our top priority is economic and social development, but we often ask ourselves: development for what and for whom? There is a growing awareness in the world that technology and intensive specialisation do not necessarily enrich the human dimension. The urgent need is for a unified view of the world's resources and the world's experience, and of man's power of invention. We are one of the species on this planet Earth. Have we the right to squander its resources, to pollute water and air, to extinguish animal and plant life, to upset the delicate balance in Nature and mar its beauty? Cannot an organisation such as the United Nations direct our thinking in terms of the larger well-being?

Much has been said about the population increases and the advance of science and technology. But the more significant explosion of our times is the awakening of human consciousness on a global scale. Seers have for long thought of mankind as one family (*Vasudhaiva kutumbakam*, as ancient sages in my country called it). Modern technology has brought all countries close, and has provided visual proof of this unity. What man saw with his inward eye, science has made possible to see with the outward eye. Science, technology and art are reaching across national frontiers. So are the yearnings of peoples. From a fragmentary interpretation of human civilisation, we are moving to the threshold of a universal history of man. The theories which have dominated our age seem hardly relevant, for neither appears to provide true answers to our questions.

For centuries, vast numbers in the countries under colonial rule were apathetic and resigned. Their awakening is accompanied by expectation and impatience. These have sometimes led to the growth of populism, encouraging fascism on the one hand, and the destructive exuberance of the extreme left on the other, seeking short cuts and easy ways. We see this in several countries, including my own. An addiction to violence has grown, seeking by destruction to obliterate all that was and is. But history cannot be changed; it can be used. Neither for the weak nor for the strong is there an easy way. We believe that wrong means often distort the ends, and violence for a purpose often deteriorates to violence for its own sake. Violence is evil, but what is worse is that it breeds contempt and callousness at a time when all our senses must be specially sensitive and attuned to every nuance of the swift movements of change. Mere condemnation of discontent can lead to acts of desperation. The answer is to seek to understand and remove the causes, by initiating the process of peaceful change. Rebels and non-conformists are often the pioneers and designers of change.

The Unfinished Revolution is not confined to the poorer, developing countries. The advanced countries also have their Unfinished Revolution. We find it in the movement for women's liberation, in the revolt of young people, the ferment in the universities and the assertion of Black and Brown power.

Why do these movements remain on the periphery of the nations' activities? It is not for lack of courage or sincerity, or depth of feeling, but because each group deals with only a small part of the problem and does not view it in its entirety. If these groups were to see the larger perspective, they would soon realise that it is not they alone who have been denied emancipation in a world of free men, but that the vast majority of people are themselves prisoners of old conceptions of politics, economics and of social attitudes and functioning. If their present restlessness can be harnessed to creative purposes, they can set the pace for history and give a new direction to mankind. The change we desire, the change which must come, is not of pace, quantity or manner, but of basic quality—of what man is, of what man can be.

The concepts of freedom, democracy and justice have not remained fixed but have evolved and changed over the years. People rightly look for greater content in them and seek greater participation for themselves. Each individual wants his true self to be understood, his worth to be realised.

The coming twenty-five years in which we must lay the foundations for a larger freedom for man will make many demands on the leaders and peoples of all nations and on the administrators of the United Nations and its agencies. They have done good work in difficult conditions. It is now to be considered whether the organisational structure and procedures, and the definition of goals and duties needs reappraisal. Many suggestions have been made for the better implementation of the Articles of the United Nations Charter and of its resolutions. It is obvious that there should be a recommitment by member States to the ideals of the United Nations, but it is equally important to draw up essential new programmes which might help to avoid the mistakes of the old world.

Our independence coincided with a remarkable acceleration of communications. So from the very beginning, our foreign policy was based on the premise that in a shrinking world, there could be no place for war as an instrument of policy. The responsibility to help more than five hundred million people to fulfil their aspirations gives us a compelling interest in peace, especially with our neighbours. We have always affirmed that the way of the world should be not power but peace, not confrontation but co-operation. The world is not for destruction, it is for development. Governments and statesmen of the world, indeed citizens of all nations, need to make earnest and well considered efforts to submerge national ambitions and rivalries in the wider interest of the preservation of civilisation and the survival of humanity.

Time, space, matter, life, all the old certainties are under question. The exploration of outer space and the research into the nature of life are placing new responsibility in man's hands. Many countries are turning their attention towards the sea-bed and its treasures. The United Nations should ensure that the resources born of all these explorations are used not merely for the aggrandisement of individual nations but for the welfare of the family of man.

The irony of mankind is that we have the means, and we see the vision, but we lack the will and the trust to take the one big step forward. As the Maitri Upanishad says, "The mind is the source of all bondage, and also the source of liberation." It is by breaking through the cages of constraint that man can go forward.

In the years to come, let the United Nations strive to bring about an era of international transformation by consent, a new era of justice and peace.

6. FOREIGN AFFAIRS, 1971*

Usually, when people think of India they either think of the bejewelled fabulous maharajas, or of the abject poverty of the people. Or they think that we are idealists whose philosophy has not much relevance to the realities of the day. Perhaps all this is true but it is only a very small part of the picture of a very vast country. It is a country which has its problems, but it is not all problems. It is a country which along with the problems

*Address to the Austrian Society for Foreign Policy and International Relations, Vienna, October 28, 1971.

has music and dancing. It has its art and culture and even amongst the poorest people you will find laughter and joy in life.

I did not really want to go into the details of Indian problems, but I think it is important that people in Austria should know something about my country, because it is of importance what happens there. It is of importance not only to Asia, but, I think, to Europe as well.

India is a land of many contradictions, existing in different centuries, people strongly asserting themselves yet fearful of any fundamental change. There is a constant clash between tolerance and dogma, between the basic Indian values and the superficial habits of dress or ritual. To all this has been added the new clash which perhaps all countries face which is the struggle between the *status quo* and the forces of change.

It is customary for people to think of diversity as a disadvantage and therefore to seek to impose uniformity in the search for unity and strength. In India we have found that diversity is a source of strength, that the continuity of the Indian civilisation for thirty centuries is itself due to its diversity, to its talent for absorbing new elements and tolerating differences. This is how India can have sixteen major languages and seven major religions and yet function effectively as one nation. Our religious minorities are not minorities in the sense in which the conventional nation-states of Europe have understood the word. Our minority groups are equal under the law. Our Constitution says that all religions are entitled to equal respect and equal protection. The sixty million Moslems who live in India, the fifteen million Christians, ten million Sikhs and a much smaller number of Buddhists, Jains, Zoroastrians, and so on, are equal to the 450 million Hindus. Sometimes there is tension, but government and public opinion always assert themselves to restore harmony. It is not the mere constitutional provision of equality which has made these people equal so much as the fact that in the last twenty-four years we have built a system in which people can truly participate. Our democratic structure functions not merely at the level of a national Parliament but goes down to the grass-roots level in the form of effective rural self-governing councils.

In our Fifth General Elections last March, 152 million people went to cast their votes, in spite of the fact that at least in one of our States there was grave threat of violence and all over the country there was a great deal of mischievous and false propaganda about our policies and programmes.

I would like to say that it is natural perhaps that the European should look at Indian problems from the European point of view. But we have to see the problems of Asia and Africa from the point of view of the conditions which had existed in these countries and which exist today. For instance take literacy. We are all for literacy. We are trying to expand adult literacy and we believe it is a very necessary programme. But I personally think that literacy should not be equated with the capacity to judge, or with understanding of what one wants. In our general elections, as I said just now, a great deal of effort and money were spent to divert the people's attention. But in every election the people have grown more mature, and if some have been misled by propaganda, or by factors which are irrelevant to the situation, their number is certainly not larger than happens in fully literate affluent countries.

I would like to tell a small story about democracy. In the very first elections, I visited my father's constituency. I was stopped on the road for an unscheduled meeting and I made a short speech. An old farmer got up and said, "Only yesterday we had another gentleman and he said the opposite of what you are saying. Which of you was telling the truth?" I said, "Well, obviously I cannot say that I am telling the untruth, but I am also not willing to say that the other gentleman told the untruth. We are trying to bring democracy to our country and this means that everybody says what he has to say, but you, the people, must judge who is saying what is in your interest, who is going to do what is in your interest." But the farmer said, "Do you belong to the Congress Party?" I said, "Yes." "Then you have no business to let this man speak to us and tell us lies." This was in 1950–51. But even in the next elections, one did not hear such a question or such a demand. Our people have got used to the fact that different parties put different points of view. So step by step they learn. Every election is not merely the opportunity to vote, it is an opportunity to be educated in the ways of democracy and in the policies of the different parties.

Some people say that the political unity of India is a gift of the British. In reality today's political unity is primarily the result of our movement for freedom from the British and equally the result of our subsequent success in holding together and consolidating that unity through the full functioning of democracy.

The break-up of the feudal order in Europe was accompanied by much violence and bloodshed, but in India we have been able to achieve this peacefully. There were two aspects. Firstly, there were the very big land-owners who had oppressed the people in the rural areas for many years, taken their land and so on. We abolished absentee landlordship and gave about twenty million more families the right to land-ownership. But I must confess that our land reform legislation is not adequate yet in all the States, because this is not a central, federal subject, it is a state subject. And I myself am exasperated by the slow implementation of even the land legislation which has been passed in some of the States. Nevertheless, every year we see some improvement in the situation.

The second part of the feudal order was represented by the princes. When the British withdrew, there was not only British India consisting of a dozen provinces, there were more than 500 native states where maharajas ruled with varying degrees of autocracy. In theory each could become an independent state and one or two of them did try to do so. But our leaders were able to persuade them all to merge into Indian polity without the use of force.

In order to enable the princes to get used to the new order of equality, certain transitional arrangements were made in the shape of annual payments, special privileges and so on. Recently we have decided to abolish these also, so that the disparities and unearned privileges can be further diminished.

The reorganisation of the constituent states in India provides a good insight into our endeavour of converting diversity into an element of political strength. Even in small countries we see the hold of smaller regional loyalties. In a vast country these loyalties could become explosive, if the system had not taken adequate note of the legitimacy of state rights and fitted them into a pattern of the larger loyalty to the nation.

As you all know, we adopted the British parliamentary system, but with this difference, that we have a more or less federal set-up. Each voter has two votes. He gives one vote for Parliament, one vote for the State assembly. The elections are not necessarily held together. The majority party elects its leader and in the centre the leader becomes the prime minister and in the states what we call the chief minister.

In several states we have had either coalition governments or governments entirely of an opposition party. But we have maintained good relationship with these governments and we have discussed problems and programmes with each of the people concerned.

The written word of the Constitution has been strengthened through the evolution of many political conventions and institutional forums, such as the Finance Commission, the National Development Council and so on.

Of course, where there are men (and of course also women) there are bound to be tensions, and now and then they become so evident that we have to set up organisations such as the National Integration Council. But this is all a part of life and in no way do these disagreements weaken our unity or interfere with our progress. We have steadily grown stronger by responding positively to genuine local demands and grievances, whether of linguistic groups or tribes wanting to retain their special identity, or demands to redress imbalances caused by the uneven economic development of a region. The political importance of tolerance is borne out by the history of the constituent states of India. Tolerance does not mean adopting the line of least resistance but the resolution of tensions and rivalries in such a way that violence is prevented. This positive concept of change includes an increasing effort to cleanse society of old inequalities and injustices.

Much has been spoken and written about our caste system. Some castes were regarded as low and the people belonging to them gradually became economically very backward. Our Constitution gives them equality. And because these backward sections form one-sixth of our population, we have provided that they should have a sixth of the membership of all our legislatures, national and states, to enable them to catch up with the rest of the community until such time as this transitional provision becomes unnecessary. In these twenty years these classes have thrown up very vocal leadership and old attitudes of inferiority are gradually going.

You know that women have made great advance. We did have a movement for women's emancipation. Its leaders were interested in education, women's health and so on. But it was our national leaders' foresight that really opened the door for women. Because they recognised that in a non-violent movement, such as ours, without half the population taking an active interest and showing their sympathy, the movement could not succeed. Mahatma Gandhi's gentle voice was strong enough to persuade our women to come out of their homes and to share the hardship, the suffering and the sacrifices of the freedom movement. And this is what today has enabled them to participate equally in the work for development. We therefore did not have to fight for our rights from or with our menfolk. We fought for freedom alongside of our men and this is the spirit in India today. Where women are working, it is not to get anything from the men or in rivalry with them, but in partnership with them to create a better India for us all.

Our development plans have these simultaneous objectives: to augment production, to achieve economic self-reliance, and to ensure that no section or part of India is left out in the cold, to reallocate the effective control over the means of production, so that there is no concentration of economic power in private hands, which would distort our political democracy, to increase modern technology, so that there is minimum economic and social dislocation; and to build a social infrastructure of a new society in terms of public health, education, vocational training and scientific research.

But our planning is not regimented. We are trying to lessen the inequalities by giving greater opportunity for the small man through special programmes. And although our aim is a socialist society we recognise the part the private sector can play in industrial production.

Perhaps in a regimented society we could have made quicker economic progress. But at the same time we believe that democracy strengthens the people and therefore the results of what is achieved are more stable and have more lasting effect on society.

In order to give you some idea of what has been achieved through the experiment of democratic planning I would like to give you some figures. In 1951 our production of foodgrains was 55 million tonnes. This year it has been 108 million tonnes and we are today fully self-sufficient in foodgrains. We do not have to import them, except now for this very large question of the refugees. Similarly in steel and other industrial sectors, production has trebled and has become greatly diversified. In 1951 the number of school-going children was 23·5 million. Today it is 83 million.

In foreign policy we have adopted what is known as non-alignment. This policy is not identical with Austria's policy of neutralism. Non-alignment to us did not mean being neutral or unconcerned with what was happening or even not having relationships with countries of the military blocs. It merely meant that we would not join a military bloc and we would not be guided by any other country. That is, we reserve the right to judge each international issue on its merits and keeping in view our national interests and interest of world peace. And we feel that this policy has served us well and we feel that in the context of our recent history it continues to be necessary and beneficial and that it will give us strength to meet the challenges that confront us internationally.

Naturally the question arises whether our signing a treaty of peace, friendship and co-operation with the Soviet Union has affected this policy. Many people are saying in the newspapers that it has affected that policy. But we do not think so. In fact one of the clauses of the treaty specifically mentions that the Soviet Union acknowledges India's policy of non-alignment and that the treaty will not interfere with it. And President Tito, who is one of the co-founders of the non-aligned group and who feels most personally concerned with non-alignment, has also said that he understands the situation and that he agrees that it does not touch our non-alignment. Although we have had friendship with the Soviet Union before and continue to do so, we also have friendships with other countries. Whatever decision we take on different issues will be, as I said earlier, according to how we see the situation from our national point of view.

We feel that the fundamental premises of non-alignment stand vindicated by events in other parts of the world in recent years. Compared with the situation prevailing in the last decade there is much greater mobility between the military blocs and also between the blocs and the non-aligned. In Europe the processes of detente have moved faster.

India welcomes the present steps to a detente as a vindication of our own conviction that the realities of the world today are basically different and that the world can survive and prosper not through confrontation but through co-operation.

During my visit to Austria I have been reminded by several people of the part which my father played in the signing of the Austrian State Treaty. At that time he happened to be first in Austria and then in Switzerland and the then Foreign Minister, I think it was Mr. Gruber, sent a message to him asking him whether he could send a message to Mr. Khrushchev to say that Austria was ready for such a treaty and I believe that what he did then did help in a small measure to make the treaty possible.

All of you here are aware of the serious situation which has developed in the last seven months on our borders. Perhaps you know that the two parts of Pakistan are divided by a thousand miles of Indian territory. But that is no reason for the two parts not to get on. Why the situation arose was because the legitimate grievances of the people of East Bengal were not attended to in time. When the election took place, Sheikh Mujibur Rahman, who was the leader of the Awami Party, had a six-point prog-ramme. It included greater autonomy for East Bengal but it did not ask for independence or secession. They wanted to have better relations with India but not at the cost of Pakistan. All that they wanted was trade with India because the economy of East Pakistan had suffered greatly since this trade was stopped.

This programme was public and the election was fought on the basis of this programme and under the present regime. So one cannot say that anything underhand or hidden was done. But when Sheikh Mujibur Rahman won the elections with the biggest majority that any election has given a national leader, there seems to have been some rethinking on the part of the government.

One more thing I would like to point out. This is not a question of a minority wanting something from a majority. When you take the whole of Pakistan together, the people of East Bengal are in the majority. So, instead of democracy following its normal course, the period of negotiations saw the bringing over of more troops and the unleashing of a reign of terror such as has seldom been seen in the world. This is what has led to about 13 per cent of the entire population of East Bengal leaving their homes and trying to take shelter in India. The size of the refugee population is about the size of your own country here. Among the victims are Hindus, Muslims, Christians and Buddhists. In the beginning the special victims of the persecution were scholars, authors and university men. We are told by people who have come from the other side that on the night of March 25, which was a Thursday, a special attack was made on Dacca University and over 300 people—students, faculty members and others—were killed.

Through the centuries India has offered refuge to the persecuted but this time the problem is different in size and character. The tensions created in our country are political and social not less than economic but you can imagine what the economic burden is of looking after such a vast number of people. The threat to our security and stability is also very real.

Our progress has sharpened our people's impatience. It is not true to say that the poor are poorer, because even the poor have advanced a bit. But it is true that they see their poverty with much sharper eyes. It is true that they are not prepared to wait any longer. We have taken the path of socialism because we feel there cannot be real democracy if there is a very great economic inequality. Even though the Constitution gives equal rights, if a very large part of the population is not able to benefit from what the Constitution gives them, then democracy cannot be complete. So if India cannot maintain its stability, I think it does threaten Asia and it does threaten world peace as well. Governmental and parliamentary leaders from many countries have shown understanding of the issues involved, but many others are acting, may I say, somewhat with lack of insight.

7. NATIONAL PRESS CLUB, WASHINGTON, 1971*

I was here just five years ago and I spoke to you then of what we have been trying to do in India. Much has happened in this time, not only in India but in all parts of the world. But naturally, just now I am more concerned with my own country.

Doubts were expressed then in 1966, in my own country and by the world press, including the press in the United States, about our unity, our democracy and even our ability to survive. Well, all I can say is there I am again. But we have gone through a period of darkness and difficulty, which even for a people accustomed to hardship has been exceptionally severe. We are now self-sufficient in wheat and rice and other cereals, which are the staple diet of our people. With increasing expansion in irrigation facilities and fertiliser output, major breakthroughs are expected in other farm products as well. Our family planning programmes have had some impact. The census held this last March showed that our population was fourteen million less than had been estimated.

Political changes in our party have taken place peacefully, giving greater coherence and sense of direction to our national life. Our confidence in our people was justified in our general election. On an average, sixty per cent of the people voted, not only in the cities but in the remote areas of the interior and in the mountains. The people gave me and my party a good majority. But what was special about the elections was the enthusiasm with which the people, and especially the young people, made it their own campaign.

The elections aroused new hope in our people and generated new energy and purpose in us. But today your thoughts and mine are pre-occupied with the crisis of Bangla Desh, that is, East Bengal. There, too,

*Address to the National Press Club, Washington, November 5, 1971.

elections were held. The fact that even under a military regime the people of East Bengal so overwhelmingly voted for the Awami League showed their deep desire for democratic rights. The military rulers used the period of negotiations to amass troops. And on the very day when the Awami League thought that settlement was to be reached, a reign of terror such as history has rarely witnessed was unleashed.

I have not hesitated sometimes to criticise the press, of course, in self-defence. But on this occasion, I should like to express appreciation of the manner in which the press correspondents of many countries have tried to arouse the conscience of the world. They have shown courage and perseverance in lifting the veil around East Bengal and revealing the truth of the grim tragedy being enacted there. Their words have been honest and direct, but the photographs have outdone them in conveying the very essence of sorrow and misery.

What is taking place there is not a civil war, in the ordinary sense of the word; it is a genocidal punishment of civilians for having voted democratically. It is a strange and cynical way of getting rid of one's opponents and of deliberately using helpless millions as a weapon against a neighbour nation. The number of the refugees is equal to the population of some of the countries of Europe, such as Austria and Belgium, where I was only recently.

We feel that this is a new kind of aggression. It certainly casts an unconscionable economic burden on us and has created political and social tensions endangering our security. This is not a purely internal matter of one country, because the overflow of the political, economic and security consequences are affecting another country, that is, India. This is not an international dispute, certainly not an Indo-Pakistani dispute, for the traditional international instruments to be invoked.

We are told that the confrontation of troops is a threat to peace. Is there no threat to peace when a whole people are massacred? Will the world be concerned only if people die because of war between two countries and not if hundreds of thousands are butchered and expelled by a military regime waging war against the people?

We cannot draw upon precedents to deal with this unprecedented variety of aggression. We have to devise new patterns of response. It is in order to impress on world leaders the nature of the crisis and the means of resolving it that I wrote to heads of government several months ago and sent some of my colleagues to meet them. We informed them that the only way out of the mess which the military rulers of Pakistan have made for themselves is to have a political settlement with the elected representatives of East Bengal, Sheikh Mujibur Rahman, if he is alive, and his colleagues who embody the will of the people.

Had the world realised it then, much of this mounting misery and the migration of many more millions could have been avoided. The chances of such a settlement have grown more slender with each new day of neglect. But there might still be time if world leaders appreciated the reality of the situation.

In the various capitals I have visited on this tour I have been asked what solution India would like. The question is not what we would like, or what one or other of the big powers would like, but what the people of East Bengal will accept and what solution would be a lasting one.

I should like to plead with the world not to press me for a solution which leaves out the people of East Bengal. It is an illusion to think that the fate of a country can be decided without reference to its people. Once again, we see the old habit of underestimating the power of nationalism in Asia and of the demand of the people of Asia to make their own choice. Those who subscribe to the belief that democratically reached decisions are the most viable should recognise that the process of democracy admits no geographical disqualification. If democracy is good for you, it is good for us in India, and it is good for the people of East Bengal.

The suppression of democracy is the original cause of all the trouble in Pakistan. The nations of the world should make up their minds who is more important to them, one man and his machine or a whole nation.

I am asked what initiatives India will take. We have taken the biggest possible initiative in remaining so self-restrained and in keeping in check the anger within our country. We have endeavoured strenuously to see that this does not become an Indo-Pakistan issue. Any direct talks between the two countries would immediately be converted into such a dispute and make the solution more difficult. Pakistan has been trying to create conditions in which the world would think that Pakistan is threatened by a more powerful neighbour. As I have said, the threat to Pakistan has come from its own rulers, not from us. When the regime there found out that its calculations did not succeed, it moved its troops to our western frontier, knowing full well that we would be forced to follow suit.

Pakistan's pleas for observers from the United Nations, for bilateral talks with India, and for mutual withdrawal of troops seemed very plausible at first sight. But these are only methods to divert the attention of the world from the root of the problem to what are merely byproducts. We cannot be sidetracked. We cannot have a dialogue with Pakistan on the future of East Bengal, because we have no right to speak for the people of East Bengal. Only Sheikh Mujib or the elected and accepted representatives of East Bengal have that right.

I have merely touched on certain points and on what I thought would interest you the most. But I want to add only one thing, because the President of your club said that I had come here to ask for aid. I have not asked for any aid, neither in this country nor in any of the other countries which I have visited. I believe that it is not the task of any one country to say to another what they should do, even if it is a question of helping. It is my duty to put the situation in my country and its neighbourhood, to give my assessment of the situation to the leaders of the countries I visit. It is for them, then, with their own assessment and what they hear from me, to make up their mind what they think about this and what they should do about it.

CHAPTER SEVEN

Indo-Pakistan War and the Birth of Bangla Desh, 1971

1. INTRODUCTION

WHEN PAKISTAN CAME INTO BEING IN 1947 ON THE END OF BRITISH rule over India, it consisted of two wings separated by nearly a thousand miles. Even in the first few years, Bengali-speaking East Pakistan, which accounted for more than half of the country's population, began to feel that it was denied its legitimate share of political power. During the long years of army rule to which Pakistan was subjected, there was a growing demand for autonomy among the people of the eastern wing. When the country's first general elections were held in 1970, the Awami League, led by Sheikh Mujibur Rahman, won an overwhelming victory. The West Pakistan military rulers felt that by virtue of his majority, Sheikh Mujibur Rahman would stake a claim to the country's prime ministership. Under cover of negotiations with the Sheikh, they made preparations to annul the results of the election. On March 23, 1971, Sheikh Mujibur Rahman was arrested and a reign of terror was unleashed. So brutal was the punishment meted out to the people of the region by the military regime that they were completely alienated from Pakistan. The demand for autonomy became transformed into a firm resolve to establish an independent Bangla Desh. Those leaders who could escape the repression formed a government in exile.

A very large number of men, women and children fled from genocide and sought shelter in India. More than ten million people crossed over in eight months. At incalculable strain to her economic and administrative resources, India opened a vast network of camps to give them shelter, food and medicines. Indira Gandhi urged the international community to stop this flood and prevail upon the rulers of Pakistan to reach a settlement with the people of Bangla Desh. She undertook a mission of persuasion to many world capitals, but little came out of it.

Meanwhile internal opposition to the Pakistan army grew within Bangla Desh to the proportions of a resistance movement, which was spearheaded by the Mukti Bahini. Pakistan alleged that India was supporting the Mukti Bahini. On December 3, 1971, the President of Pakistan, General Yahya Khan, ordered the bombing of major Indian airfields. The Bangla Desh crisis was thus converted into full-scale war on the eastern and western borders of India.

Thirteen days later, on December 16, 1971, the Pakistani forces in the east surrendered to a joint command of Indian and Bangla Desh forces. After announcing that "Dacca is now the free capital of a free country", Indira Gandhi unilaterally offered a cease-fire in the western sector. It came into effect on December 17, 1971.

2. PRIME MINISTER'S BROADCAST TO THE NATION*

I speak to you at a moment of grave peril to our country and to our people. Some hours ago, soon after 5.30 p.m. on December 3, Pakistan launched a full-scale war against us. The Pakistani Air Force suddenly struck at our airfields in Amritsar, Pathankot, Srinagar, Avantipur, Uttarlai, Jodhpur, Ambala and Agra. Their ground forces are shelling our defence positions in Sulaimanki, Khemkaran, Poonch and other sectors.

Since last March, we have borne the heaviest burden and withstood the greatest pressure, in a tremendous effort to urge the world to help in bringing about a peaceful solution and preventing the annihilation of an entire people, whose only crime was to vote for democracy. But the world ignored the basic causes and concerned itself only with certain repercussions. The situation was bound to deteriorate and the courageous band of freedom fighters have been staking their all in defence of the values for which we also have struggled, and which are basic to our way of life.

Today the war in Bangla Desh has become a war on India; this has imposed upon me, my Government and the people of India a great responsibility. We have no other option but to put our country on a war

*From New Delhi, in the early hours of December 4, 1971.

footing. Our brave officers and *jawans* are at their post mobilised for the defence of the country. An emergency has been declared for the whole of India. Every necessary step is being taken, and we are prepared for all eventualities.

I have no doubt that it is the united will of our people that this wanton and unprovoked aggression should be decisively and finally repelled. In this resolve, the Government is assured of the full and unflinching support of all political parties and every Indian citizen. We must be prepared for a long period of hardship and sacrifice.

We are a peace-loving people. But we know that peace cannot last if we do not guard our democracy and our way of life. So today we fight not merely for territorial integrity but for the basic ideals which have given strength to this country and on which alone we can progress to a better future.

Aggression must be met, and the people of India will meet it with fortitude and determination and with discipline and utmost unity.

3. OPEN LETTER TO MR. RICHARD NIXON*

I am writing at a moment of deep anguish at the unhappy turn which the relations between our two countries have taken.

I am setting aside all pride, prejudice and passion and trying, as calmly as I can, to analyse once again the origins of the tragedy which is being enacted.

There are moments in history when brooding tragedy and its dark shadows can be lightened by recalling great moments of the past. One such great moment which has inspired millions of people to die for liberty was the Declaration of Independence by the United States of America. That Declaration stated that whenever any form of Government became destructive of man's inalienable rights to life, liberty and the pursuit of happiness, it was the right of the people to alter or abolish it.

All unprejudiced persons objectively surveying the grim events in Bangla Desh since March 25 have recognised the revolt of 75 million people, a people who were forced to the conclusion that neither their life, nor their liberty, to say nothing of the possibility of the pursuit of

*Open letter to President Nixon, written on December 15, 1971.

happiness, was available to them. The world press, radio and television have faithfully recorded the story. The most perceptive of American scholars who are knowledgeable about the affairs of this sub-continent revealed the anatomy of East Bengal's frustrations.

The tragic war, which is continuing, could have been averted if, during the nine months prior to Pakistan's attack on us on December 3, the great leaders of the world had paid some attention to the fact of revolt, tried to see the reality of the situation and searched for a genuine basis for reconciliation. I wrote letters along these lines. I undertook a tour in quest of peace at a time when it was extremely difficult to leave the country in the hope of presenting to some of the leaders of the world the situation as I saw it. It was heart-breaking to find that while there was sympathy for the poor refugees, the disease itself was ignored.

War could also have been avoided if the power, influence and authority of all the States, and above all of the United States, had got Sheikh Mujibur Rahman released. Instead, we were told that a civilian administration was being installed. Everyone knows that this civilian administration was a farce; today the farce has turned into a tragedy.

Lip service was paid to the need for a political solution, but not a single worthwhile step was taken to bring this about. Instead, the rulers of West Pakistan went ahead holding farcical elections to seats which had been arbitrarily declared vacant.

There was not even a whisper that anyone from the outside world had tried to have contact with Mujibur Rahman. Our earnest plea that Sheikh Mujibur Rahman should be released, or that, even if he were to be kept under detention, contact with him might be established, was not considered practical on the ground that the U.S. could not urge policies which might lead to the overthrow of President Yahya Khan. While the United States recognised that Mujibur was a core factor in the situation and that unquestionably in the long run Pakistan must acquiesce in the direction of greater autonomy for East Pakistan, arguments were advanced to demonstrate the fragility of the situation and of Yahya Khan's difficulty.

Mr. President, may I ask you in all sincerity: Was the release or even secret negotiations with a single human being, namely, Sheikh Mujibur Rahman, more disastrous than the waging of a war?

The fact of the matter is that the rulers of West Pakistan got away with the impression that they could do what they liked because no one, not even the United States, would choose to take a public position that while

Pakistan's integrity was certainly sacrosanct, human rights, liberty were no less so and that there was a necessary inter-connection between the inviolability of States and the contentment of their people.

Mr. President, despite the continued defiance by the rulers of Pakistan of the most elementary facts of life, we would still have tried our hardest to restrain the mounting pressure as we had for nine long months, and war could have been prevented had the rulers of Pakistan not launched a massive attack on us by bombing our airfields in Amritsar, Pathankot, Srinagar, Avantipur, Uttarlai, Jodhpur, Ambala and Agra in the broad daylight on December 3, 1971 at a time when I was away in Calcutta, my colleague, the Defence Minister, was in Patna and was due to leave further for Bangalore in the South and another senior colleague of mine, the Finance Minister, was in Bombay. The fact that this initiative was taken at this particular time of our absence from the capital showed perfidious intentions. In the face of this, could we simply sit back trusting that the rulers of Pakistan or those who were advising them had peaceful, constructive and reasonable intent?

We are asked what we want. We seek nothing for ourselves. We do not want any territory of what was East Pakistan and now constitutes Bangla Desh. We do not want any territory of West Pakistan. We do want lasting peace with Pakistan. But will Pakistan give up its ceaseless and yet pointless agitation of the last twenty-four years over Kashmir? Are they willing to give up their hate campaign and posture of perpetual hostility towards India? How many times in the last twenty-four years have my father and I offered a Pact of Non-aggression to Pakistan? It is matter of recorded history that each time such offer was made, Pakistan rejected it out of hand.

We are deeply hurt by the innuendos and insinuations that it was we who have precipitated the crisis and have in any way thwarted the emergence of solutions. I do not really know who is responsible for this calumny. During my visit to the United States, United Kingdom, France, Germany, Austria and Belgium, the point I emphasised, publicly as well as privately, was the immediate need for a political settlement. We waited nine months for it. When Dr. Kissinger came in July 1971, I had emphasised to him the importance of seeking an early political settlement. But we have not received, even to this day, the barest framework of a settlement which would take into account the facts as they are and not as we imagine them to be.

Be that as it may, it is my earnest and sincere hope that with all the knowledge and deep understanding of human affairs you, as President of the United States and reflecting the will, the aspirations and idealism of the great American people, will at least let me know where precisely we have gone wrong before your representatives or spokesmen deal with us with such harshness of language.

4. PRIME MINISTER'S STATEMENT*

I have an announcement to make. The West Pakistan forces have unconditionally surrendered in Bangla Desh. The instrument of surrender was signed in Dacca at 16.31 hours I.S.T. today by Lieutenent-General A. A. K. Niazi on behalf of the Pakistan Eastern Command. Lieutenant-General Jagjit Singh Aurora, G.O.C.-in-C. of the Indian and Bangla Desh forces in the Eastern Theatre accepted the surrender. Dacca is now the free capital of a free country.

This House and the entire nation rejoice in this historic event. We hail the people of Bangla Desh in their hour of triumph. We hail the brave young men and boys of the Mukti Bahini for their valour and dedication. We are proud of our own Army, Navy, Air Force and the Border Security Force, who have so magnificently demonstrated their quality and capacity. Their discipline and devotion to duty are well known. India will remember with gratitude the sacrifices of those who have laid down their lives, and our thoughts are with their families.

Our Armed Forces are under strict orders to treat Pakistani prisoners of war in accordance with the Geneva Convention and to deal with all sections of the population of Bangla Desh in a humane manner. The Commanders of the Mukti Bahini have issued similar orders to their forces. Although the Government of Bangla Desh have not yet been given an opportunity to sign the Geneva Convention, they also have declared that they will fully abide by it. It will be the responsibility of the Government of Bangla Desh, the Mukti Bahini and the Indian Armed Forces to prevent any reprisals.

Our objectives were limited—to assist the gallant people of Bangla Desh and their Mukti Bahini to liberate their country from a reign of

*Statement made in Parliament, New Delhi, December 16, 1971.

terror and to resist aggression on our own land. Indian Armed Forces will not remain in Bangla Desh any longer than is necessary.

The millions who were driven out of their homes across our borders have already begun trekking back. The rehabilitation of this war-torn land calls for dedicated team work by its Government and people.

We hope and trust that the father of this new nation, Sheikh Mujibur Rahman, will take his rightful place among his own people and lead Bangla Desh to peace, progress and prosperity. The time has come when they can together look forward to a meaningful future in their Sonar Bangla.* They have our good wishes.

The triumph is not theirs alone. All nations who value the human spirit will recognise it as a significant milestone in man's quest for liberty.

*Means "golden Bengal".

5. CEASE-FIRE ON WESTERN FRONT†

On March 31, 1971, six days after the great upheaval in Bangla Desh, I had the honour to move a Resolution in this House.

I said then that India's permanent interest in peace and our commitment to uphold and defend human rights demanded the immediate cessation of the use of force and of the massacre of the defenceless people of Bangla Desh. I had called upon all peoples and Governments to take urgent and constructive steps to prevail upon the Government of Pakistan to immediately end the systematic decimation of a people.

I had concluded my statement by expressing the profound conviction of this House that the historic upsurge of the 75 million people of East Bengal would triumph. We also gave an assurance that their struggle and sacrifice would receive the wholehearted sympathy and support of the people of India.

Today the pledge we then made together in this House and in the country stands redeemed.

It is natural that the people of India should be elated. We can also understand the great rejoicing of the people of Bangla Desh. I share the elation and the joy. But as the Gita says, neither joy nor sorrow should tilt the balance of our equanimity or blur our vision of the future.

†Statement made in Parliament, New Delhi, December 17, 1971.

All those who have borne arms, all those who have been involved in the planning and direction of the operations, all the people of India who have responded so generously—these are to be thanked and congratulated.

It is a victory but a victory not only of arms but of ideals. The Mukti Bahini could not have fought so daringly but for its passionate urge for freedom and the establishment of a special identity of Bangla Desh. Our own forces could not have been so fearless and relentless had they not been convinced of their cause.

India has stood for breadth of vision, tolerance of the points of view of others, of being in the battle, yet above it.

We stand for democracy, for secularism and for socialism. Only this combination opens the way for full freedom, gives protection to the weaker sections and the opportunity for the growth of different personalities. We believe that no nation can be built on concepts which are negative or which do not have meaning for all its people. Unfortunately, Pakistan had based its policies on hatred for and confrontation with India.

While we re-dedicate ourselves to our ideals, I hope the people of Pakistan will seek a path which is more in keeping with their circumstances and needs. These twenty-four years we have heard many aggressive speeches and much abusive and false propaganda against us. We cannot believe that this is the true voice of the Pakistani people. They have been kept in darkness by their successive regimes.

We want to assure them that we have no enmity towards them. There are more things in common than those which divide us. We should like to fashion our relations with the people of Pakistan on the basis of friendship and understanding. Let them live as masters in their own house and devote their energies to the removal of poverty and inequalities in their country.

It is this sincere desire which prompted us last evening to instruct our Army, Navy and Air Force to cease operations from 20.00 hours today on all fronts in the West.

I am grateful for the support which all political parties of the country have given throughout this difficult period and specially to this initiative on behalf of peace.

This offer was communicated to the world community by our Minister of External Affairs, Sardar Swaran Singh, in New York. We also had it formally conveyed to the Government of Pakistan through the Swiss

Embassy. We hope that the people and rulers of Pakistan will appreciate and reciprocate this offer.

The consequences which flow from a failure to do so will rest squarely upon the military rulers of Pakistan. However, regardless of what happens on the Western front, let us not be complacent. The coming months specially will bring new and complex problems. We must be ever vigilant to safeguard our integrity and our interests, and above all the fundamental beliefs of our national existence.

CHAPTER EIGHT

Speeches, 1971–1972

1. DEMOCRACY IN INDIA*

DURING OUR STRUGGLE FOR INDEPENDENCE, IT SEEMED THAT freedom itself would be fulfilment. But, when we achieved it we knew that every completion was a beginning. For us, this was a start of a great experiment in the creation of democracy in an ancient, complex and vast country.

The story of Indian development is not without significance for the rest of the world. How could it be otherwise when it encompasses the aspirations and struggles of over 550,000,000 human beings? Political theorists with their neatly labelled indices have sometimes spoken of democracy in India as a futile quest. To them, democracy could only be a two-party system worked by those who were educated in a particular way. Perhaps as advanced people of the West a generation ago protested that the colonial countries were not ready for freedom, so it was said that the under-developed societies of Asia and Africa were not ready for democracy, and could achieve order only under dictatorship of some kind or, at most, a controlled or guided democracy. Can democracy be guided any more than freedom? Is not a guided democracy a contradiction? Perhaps these questions are irrelevant. For it now seems that in some countries the word "democracy" was used as a shield for reaction and the subversion of freedom. But we did take democracy seriously. To us it conveyed the equality of all people to participate at every level in the development of their country and the functioning of government.

In the choice of political institutions, it is not inevitably the past that is decisive, but the changing conditions of the lives and attitudes of people

*Address to the Royal Institute of International Affairs, Chatham House, London, October 29, 1971.

and the capacity of those who are in positions of leadership to involve the largest number of people in the political process.

The British ruled over us for two hundred years. Little did those early colonisers realise that along with their flag they brought the seeds which would destroy their rule. Macaulay, who pleaded so passionately for Western education, did not quite realise that he was undermining the edifice he was so anxious to perpetuate. The nineteenth and twentieth centuries brought ancient India face to face with the imperatives of the contemporary world. And we quickly absorbed all that was relevant and significant in Bentham and Mill, in Rousseau and Voltaire down to Marx and Weber. And all this was grafted on to the Indian sub-continent. And we then had Tagore, Gandhi and Nehru to mention only a few.

Our democracy is dedicated to planned economic development, the peaceful transformation of an old social order and the uplifting of millions of people from conditions of social, economic and technological under-development. Thus, what we are attempting in India is not mere imitation of the Westminster system but a creative application of a meaningful democracy to the vastly different economic and social problems of India.

Democracy was not entirely new to us for its roots could be found also in our old *panchayat* system. This system probably came into being because the village and the people were too distant from the centres of political power. Today the ancient institution has been transformed into a new organ of self-government at district and what we call block level as a link between the Government's programme and the people.

The concept of the rule of law and the British pattern of administration may have helped to keep order in the country but much in these institutions has remained static and without changes they are becoming stumbling blocks to progress and democracy.

There are forces in our society as in others which pull in opposite directions. The competitiveness of democracy and of contemporary living seems superficially sometimes to have strengthened the hold of caste, religion and region, for these are now exploited for social and economic gain. But this is a passing phase and these differences cannot weaken India's fundamental unity nor the basic sense of Indianness which is a powerful binding factor. Paradoxical though it may sound, we believe that the functioning of democracy itself can remove these obstacles on the democratic path.

Education has expanded tremendously. Today there are 2·5 million students in colleges. The number of children in schools has gone up from 23·4 million in 1951 to 83,000,000 this year. But I am sorry to say that we have not done as well as we should in our programme for adult literacy. Without being able to read, a person's world is a limited one for he cannot share the knowledge and companionship that comes with books. We must do and we are doing more for primary education, for strengthening secondary education and for adult literacy programmes. At the same time, I cannot agree with the common belief in the West that literacy by itself gives greater wisdom or understanding. Our people, illiterate though they may sometimes be, are the inheritors of an ancient culture and philosophy which has sustained them through the vicissitudes of their long history.

Indian voters have shown extraordinary insight and understanding of what goes on around them. If some are misled by false propaganda or diverted by irrelevant factors, their number is not larger than those of their literate—even educated—counterparts in other countries. The Indian voter knows where his interests lie and has exercised his right to vote with great political sophistication in spite of the competitive political platforms of numerous parties, even in the face of threat and violence. It is because of this basic soundness of our people that democracy has taken root in India.

Since long before Independence, the Congress Party has committed itself to certain programmes. Indeed, our leaders had made it clear that we were fighting not only against foreign rule but against all that was evil in our society, against injustice and poverty and social inequality. Our system must therefore cater to the genuine needs of ordinary people without neglecting the long-term development of the country. Development adds a new dimension to the challenge of democracy.

Three distinct streams of thought have combined to produce what might vaguely be called the Indian approach to democracy. There is the stream of liberalism and parliamentary democracy, which emerged out of the British system—parliamentary institutions, political parties, free elections, fundamental rights and freedom, the rule of law, which formed the political core of our democratic system. Parliament is the commanding centre of our political system, and government's responsibility to the legislature at the centre and in the states is beyond dispute.

In modern society, freedom cannot be the unrestricted play of individualism nor the apotheosis of private interests and private enterprise as against social interest and the public good. Freedom lies in a delicate and continuous balancing of the rights of the individual with the rights of society. Our constitution and our actual political practice provide a larger degree of freedom than is obtained anywhere else in the world. We stand for the freedom of the press, but we do not accept the proposition that freedom of the press means the freedom of industrialists to own the press, or that the right of property should stand in the way of progressive and necessary social legislation to lessen glaring inequalities of wealth and bring the reality of economic freedom to larger sections of the population. We have taken action to eliminate these anomalies. We have sought to amend the Constitution in order to give substance to democracy.

The second major stream is that of socialist thought with emphasis on social democracy and economic planning and developments. Indeed the entire structure of democracy is geared to social and economic development. In Europe, democracy as we know it followed the Industrial Revolution, but in India, democracy with its freedom and pressing popular demand came first, and the process of industrialisation, economic development and major welfare schemes have to be operated in the face of diverse and contradictory pressures.

This baffling combination makes our task more difficult and because of the absence of organised propaganda our achievements appear less spectacular than the accomplishments of others by different methods. But we think that we have gained something in the longer run—not so much in glittering material terms but in terms of human values gained, in terms of human suffering avoided and in terms of the enduring and harmonious development of the individual and society. I do believe that real and lasting social transformation encompassing attitudes of mind and the ways of living of millions of people can be effective only by peaceful means.

The third stream has emanated from Mahatma Gandhi and his philosophy of non-violent revolution. The impact of Gandhian thought and method of democracy in India is indirect, impalpable, yet subtly pervasive. It has supported and enriched India. This whole experiment, this endeavour to combine freedom, socialism and the methods of peace in an immensely complex situation, is taking place in India, not in isolation from the rest of the world, but in the midst of international co-operation and in the glare of world-wide publicity. International co-operation is a constituent element of India's effort in building a progressive economy and a democratic society. This is why, ever since our independence we have put forward the idea of world peace and world co-operation, as an enlightened self-interest of India.

We believe in and have strictly adhered to the principle of non-interference. But can this be one-sided? Today, there is interference in our affairs and the stability and progress of our country are gravely threatened. As a result of the tragic events in East Bengal, 9,000,000 people have poured into our territory, creating a situation which seems to surpass the convulsions of partition. The crisis in Pakistan is a deep one and the spectre which haunts that unhappy country cannot be exorcised by the usual recourse to blaming India. Two questions arise, first, whether religion by itself can form the basis of a nation state, especially when the state machinery is impervious to the ordinary laws of political development and cultural aspirations, and secondly, whether some action other than that of the bayonet is not necessary to win loyalty. We in India are restrained and calm in the face of provocation but we are bound to protect the interest of our country.

No country, least of all one as vast and varied as India, can be classified under one label, or another. It seems to me that even those who claim expert knowledge of our country are often wide of the mark in their assessment of Indian events. Many specialists tend to fit facts into a preconceived framework of theory about caste and models of development which have no relevance to reality. Even in Britain which has such close historical ties with us, there is a wide gap in the understanding of the forces which have shaped our great history and which are influencing us today. To have a worthwhile dialogue such an understanding is vital. Britain and India must both replace old myths by a more rational approach. Given the necessary intellectual effort on both sides, I am confident that India and Britain can have creative and purposeful relations. It is the hope of bringing about such relations that brings me to London and to this Institute. Thank you for giving me this opportunity.

2. POLITICAL SCIENCE*

The relationship between one who is active in politics and those who study, analyse and comment about it is something like the relationship between an author and critics. Not all authors may like a confrontation

*Inaugural address to the thirty-third session of Indian Political Science Conference, Calcutta, December 27, 1972.

with critics, but I can assure you that I am very glad to be here this morning and to have this opportunity of meeting you, even though at some distance.

Our country is today passing through a fascinating period. People know the direction they want to take and the goal they have to reach. They are also fairly certain about their means and instruments and they have the power to wield the means and to move faster. Greater mass involvement is taking place and mass power is being generated. As I said on another occasion and in another country, this is the first time when the people are speaking for themselves. Throughout history we have had great leaders of people but the masses of the people themselves were silent. Somebody was trying to express their hopes, their aspirations and what was in their minds, as Mahatma Gandhi did so beautifully in our own times here. But for the first time today, here and all over the world, the people are coming into their own and expressing their own desires as well as their fears and difficulties.

One of the main differences between our own struggle for freedom and that of other newly-free countries is that under the leadership of Mahatma Gandhi and Jawaharlal Nehru, our movement ceased to be an elitist one and developed a mass base, while retaining high intellectual and moral sensitiveness. India, which was a cultural entity, became an independent, political reality. But the process did not stop with freedom. We have always regarded freedom not as the culmination but as the beginning—the beginning of an endeavour to fashion an integrated society in which the old divisions of caste, hierarchy and privilege are abolished and new social obligations and linkages are established involving and benefiting all sections.

Twenty-five years have passed since the attainment of freedom. In these twenty-five years, we have come far. Now and then, there may have been a slow-down and even a set-back. But, by and large, the record is that of forward movement, of consolidation and thrust. In spite of invasions from outside, in spite of drought which was the century's worst and other economic crises, the people have today more self-confidence, greater maturity and, I think, enduring faith in the system they have adopted. The quality of their judgment in successive general elections shows how our people who are far from affluent and, as the Vice-Chancellor pointed out, have no literacy even, have been politically discriminating and capable of asserting their true interests.

I should like to join issue with the Vice-Chancellor a little on that word literacy. Literacy is indeed extremely important, but the question arises: literacy for what? Once you know how to read, what are you going to read? Is it enough that we have literate people and they read what we see large masses of people in literate countries are reading? Perhaps it is better we do not read that. I do not think that literacy by itself has any connection with the growth of intelligence, the growth of judgment, or the growth of values. If there is a choice, obviously we must choose judgment and values over merely being able to make out a written word. But I entirely agree that if you can have both together, it is very much better, because that opens out the windows to the thoughts of others, to other values; it gives us the opportunity to know not only the accumulated knowledge of the past but the new knowledge which is being gained so fast all over the world. But here in India, although we are still very backward in literacy, I think our people have retained sound commonsense; they have retained a shrewd assessment of their own difficulties, conditions and the problems of their local situation and their local area. And these are the qualities which come to the surface when they have to make a decision, a political decision.

It is the people's will freely and forcefully expressed that accounts for the large degree of responsiveness in the political system and the steady removal of old prejudices and unearned privileges. It is not as if distortions have not arisen. But what is equally remarkable is the prompt endeavour at self-correction. Yet, somehow, when we read books by most of our political scientists, the writings in newspapers and periodicals, much of this excitement is missing. One gets an impression, if you will forgive the term, of unredeemed sordidness. One can understand criticism. In fact, I think it is very necessary in politics, as in all spheres of activity, and it is the duty of the scientists to weigh and evaluate. Political analysts who write on current history in Europe or America are also unsparing in their criticism of personalities, of decisions and trends, but they also manage to convey the power of forces and the fascination of the whole drama.

I have sometimes felt that not only our newspapermen but even our academic scholars fail to see the whole picture. Our system of university education and research seems to be such that we have specialists who excavate a small area without having a broad familiarity with the whole field.

When we speak about the need for change of education and the falling standards, we are not criticising the functioning of a university or all the universities. What we are saying is that education as it prevails today is not meeting the challenge of life as it is evolving. This is not merely in our country. I think it is so in most countries of the world. Like us, they are battling and struggling with this problem. Some have made a little break-through in isolated areas but there is no doubt that education as a whole has not kept pace with the discoveries and the great forces that are at work all over the world, and if we cannot give that opportunity to our young men and women, we shall not be able to go ahead and progress in the manner which we had dreamed and planned.

Another defect which comes to mind in our books on politics is the excessive use—and I think that this is something which is very important also to the thinking of intellectuals in India—of vocabulary and co-ordinates which may be valid for Western societies but are not relevant to our own conditions. In nineteenth-century Europe, when the dazzle of the Industrial Revolution was still new, the vogue arose of interpreting political systems and movements in mechanistic terms. Instead of the old metaphor about steering the ship of state, we have new metaphors of economic take-off and so on. But the style of thinking is the same old style. After Darwin expounded his theories of evolution, political scientists constructed theories of social Darwinism and this tendency has continued to our day. Most of these attempts to construct political laws on the analogy of the laws of natural sciences appear somewhat naive to me. Our own political writers have sometimes gone wrong in their forecasts and prophesies mainly because they are content to employ these derivative tools of understanding without undertaking a deeper study of the source of our own tradition and strength and the power of our own conditioning during the formative period of our national struggle and the rediscovery of our identity.

It would be wrong to think that systems work on their own. By speaking of them as self-propelling mechanisms we can commit the fallacy to which I referred earlier. It is men who run systems. When societies are highly organised, leadership might become a mere matter of management. But in our country, leadership has more than an executive role. It has to concern itself more dynamically with ideas and values and with educating the public. The people also expect a great deal more from leadership in India than they do in other countries. Nowhere are the lives of persons in politics more open to public scrutiny than in India and this again is due to the high ethical tradition that we have inherited from the days of our national struggle which was more an endeavour to build a new kind of liberated Indian than merely a fight for political independence.

It is true that not all practitioners of politics pass the test, but societies are evaluated by the quality of their aspiration as well as by the capacity of its more prominent individuals. When people speak of corruption, there is a tendency to imagine that bribery was unknown in British times. I concede that there were administrators of high rectitude then as there are now. But the entire old system, whether it was colonial rule or princely rule, was thoroughly corrupt; it does not require great acquaintance with history to know what the old empire-builders did and what they are doing today in the colonial systems which still exist. Academic scholars should help other people to have the complete picture and enable them to use knowledge as a means to improve the state of affairs and to build a better future. Merely by running down the present, we shall not be able to generate the will to correct and improve.

Many instances come to mind to illustrate what I have said about judging a thing in the correct context. You have referred to our Congress session. I saw in this morning's paper that it has been referred to as a "fair". Why is it called a fair? Because vast numbers of people come from all over the country. Why do they come? They do not come for enjoyment. They come for discussions; they come to meet each other. And I can tell you that any political party in the world would give anything it could to have such a fair in their countries and they have said so. In every country I have visited, they ask me: "How do you manage to have this sort of session?" But to some of our people it is a matter for derision, for fun. They cannot appreciate what moves a party, what moves an entire people, and if you cannot appreciate it, then you are not part of the people. Then you are somewhere in your ivory towers; you have no contact with what is happening, and therefore you will never be able to judge the situation.

It is an old question whether history has a purpose and whether science has a purpose. Their purpose is to enlarge knowledge, and the purpose of knowledge is to increase the will and the capacity to act—to act on behalf of justice and human welfare. To my mind, political science is not a fragmentary science but a total one. It cannot be content with the study of political systems and theories. It involves an understanding of psychology and ethics, of sociological and economic forces, of law and the phenomonal development of technology. In all countries of the world, the people are becoming politically active. Vast sections of the population who had been content to accept the rules laid down for them by others are today astir and insisting on full participation in the political process.

I began the speech by saying that India is passing through a fascinating period. Perhaps humanity as a whole is passing through an extraordinarily important phase which is as full of dangers as of possibilities. The insights of political science can help us to avoid some of the dangers and realise some of the possibilities. But as has been said, if you see no gods, it is because you harbour none. Or to give a more down-to-earth example, something that I read a couple of days ago on the old saying that no man is a hero to his valet. Somebody's comment on that is: "Not because the man is not a hero, but because the valet is a valet."

So let us try and look at the problems of this country and other countries from the appropriate angles. You cannot judge what is happening in India from a British, an American, a French, Japanese or any other angle. You have to understand what India has been, what India is, what makes the Indian what he is, what gives this feeling of Indianness. Time and again why should we be asked: Will democracy last in India? Will unity be maintained? I do not think any of these questions occur to the average Indian. He takes these things for granted. He knows we have this Indianness. And the last year has amply proved, if proof were necessary, that any crisis, whether it is a natural calamity, whether it is aggression, has evoked this tremendous unity, this desire to co-operate, to help one another, to make the country strong. Of course, work in peace-time is not so glamorous or spectacular, and therefore, there is a retreat, rather, there is a covering over of that overwhelming unity, and many of the daily differences, quarrels and so on have an opportunity to raise their heads. But this does not change the fundamental character of the country and the people.

Similarly, when we speak of democracy, we are always comparing it with how it functions in America or other countries. What do we care how they function there? We are making our democracy here. Our democracy has to answer the questions of the Indian people. We do not want it to be compared with any other country and it will never work if we do. We do not know if their democracy is good for them in the way they work it. But certainly for us to try and model our system on systems which have obtained or are obtaining today in other countries makes no sense to me at all. Is democracy to be what it was when the word first came into being in Greece or somewhere? What stage do you take it to? Are you going to change it as the West changes? Whatever we want to do here in India has to be done in the context of our conditions and we have to understand that our conditions are not of now. They are an outcome of thousands of years of history. While we want to change much in the old, nobody can entirely wipe out history, either one's personal history or a country's history, or the many things that have gone to form a society, its values, its thinking, even its fears.

So we have to see Indian problems and Indian developments in this context. Only then can we get a true picture and the whole picture. Obviously not all of it is a good picture. There are many fine achievements, there are many fine qualities, but there are also many faults and weaknesses. But we cannot deal with the faults, the weaknesses and the shortcomings unless we are aware also of the other side of the c in, of the achievement and all that is of value.

Indian philosophy has given us a direction. Our politics is not divorced from Indian philosophy or Indian tradition. It is not divorced from the art of India, the music of India. All these together are what make our country and to understand it you have to have some understanding of all these aspects. My father spent his lifetime trying to understand India and finally he wrote a book *The Discovery of India*, but he said at the end of it that he had unveiled only a very small part of India as it was. The quest is endless. So it is only in that spirit of trying to understand that, I think, political science can have any meaning to the student of today, the student who wants not only to think and to analyse, but to use his analysis and his thought for action, for participating in the great adventure of building a new India.

3. HUMAN ENVIRONMENT*

I have had the good fortune of growing up with a sense of kinship with Nature in all its manifestations. Birds, plants, stones were companions and, sleeping under the star-strewn sky, I became familiar with the names and movements of the constellations. But my deep interest in this our "only earth" was not for itself but as a fit home for man.

*Address to the Plenary Session of the United Nations Conference on human Environment at Stockholm, June 14, 1972.

One cannot be truly human and civilised unless one looks upon not only all fellow-men but all creation with the eyes of a friend. Throughout India, edicts carved on rocks and iron pillars are reminders that twenty-two centuries ago the Emperor Ashoka defined a king's duty as not merely to protect citizens and punish wrongdoers but also to preserve animal life and forest trees. Ashoka was the first and perhaps the only monarch until very recently to forbid the killing of a large number of species of animals for sport or food, foreshadowing some of the concerns of this Conference. He went further, regretting the carnage of his military conquests and enjoining upon his successors to find "their only pleasure in the peace that comes through righteousness".

Along with the rest of mankind, we in India—in spite of Ashoka—have been guilty of wanton disregard for the sources of our sustenance. We share your concern at the rapid deterioration of flora and fauna. Some of our own wild life has been wiped out, miles of forests with beautiful old trees, mute witnesses of history, have been destroyed. Even though our industrial development is in its infancy, and at its most difficult stage, we are taking various steps to deal with incipient environmental imbalances. The more so because of our concern for the human being—a species which is also imperilled. In poverty he is threatened by malnutrition and disease, in weakness by war, in richness by the pollution brought about by his own prosperity.

It is sad that in country after country, progress should become synonymous with an assault on Nature. We who are a part of Nature and dependent on her for every need, speak constantly about "exploiting" Nature. When the highest mountain in the world was climbed in 1953, Jawaharlal Nehru objected to the phrase "conquest of Everest" which he thought was arrogant. Is it surprising that this lack of consideration and the constant need to prove one's superiority should be projected onto our treatment of our fellow men? I remember Edward Thompson, a British writer and a good friend of India, once telling Mr. Gandhi that wild life was fast disappearing. Remarked the Mahatma—"It is decreasing in the jungles but it is increasing in the towns!"

We are gathered here under the aegis of the United Nations. We are supposed to belong to the same family sharing common traits and impelled by the same basic desires, yet we inhabit a divided world.

How can it be otherwise? There is still no recognition of the equality of man or respect for him as an individual. In matters of colour and race, religion and custom, society is governed by prejudice. Tensions arise because of man's aggressiveness and notions of superiority. The power of the big stick prevails and it is used not in favour of fair play or beauty, but to chase imaginary windmills—to assume the right to interfere in the affairs of others, and to arrogate authority for action which would not normally be allowed. Many of the advanced countries of today have reached their present affluence by their domination over other races and countries, the exploitation of their own masses and their own natural resources. They got a head start through sheer ruthlessness, undisturbed by feelings of compassion or by abstract theories of freedom, equality or justice. The stirrings of demands for the political rights of citizens, and the economic rights of the toiler came after considerable advance had been made. The riches and the labour of the colonised countries played no small part in the industrialisation and prosperity of the West. Now, as we struggle to create a better life for our people, it is in vastly different circumstances, for obviously in today's eagle-eyed watchfulness, we cannot indulge in such practices even for a worthwhile purpose. We are bound by our own ideals. We owe allegiance to the principles of the rights of workers and the norms enshrined in the charters of international organisations. Above all, we are answerable to the millions of politically awakened citizens in our countries. All these make progress costlier and more complicated.

On the one hand the rich look askance at our continuing poverty. On the other they warn us against their own methods. We do not wish to impoverish the environment any further and yet we cannot for a moment forget the grim poverty of large numbers of people. Are not poverty and need the greatest polluters? For instance, unless we are in a position to provide employment and purchasing power for the daily necessities of the tribal people and those who live in or around our jungles, we cannot prevent them from combing the forest for food and livelihood, from poaching and from despoiling the vegetation. When they themselves feel deprived, how can we urge the preservation of animals? How can we speak to those who live in villages and in slums about keeping the oceans, the rivers and the air clean when their own lives are contaminated at the source? The environment cannot be improved in conditions of poverty. Nor can poverty be eradicated without the use of science and technology.

Must there be conflict between technology and a truly better world or between enlightenment of the spirit and a higher standard of living? Foreigners sometimes ask what to us seems a very strange question, whether progress in India would not mean a diminishing of her spirituality or her values. Is spiritual quality so superficial as to be dependent upon the lack of material comfort? As a country we are no more or less spiritual than any other but traditionally our people have respected the spirit of detachment and renunciation. Historically, our great spiritual discoveries were made during periods of comparative affluence. The doctrines of detachment from possessions were developed not as rationalisation of deprivation but to prevent comfort and ease from dulling the senses. Spirituality means the enrichment of the spirit, the strengthening of one's inner resources and the stretching of one's range of experience. It is the ability to be still in the midst of activity and vibrantly alive in moments of calm; to separate the essence from circumstances; to accept joy and sorrow with some equanimity. Perception and compassion are the marks of true spirituality.

I am reminded of an incident in one of our tribal areas. The vociferous demand of elder tribal chiefs that their customs should be left undisturbed found support from noted anthropologists. In its anxiety that the majority should not submerge the many ethnical, racial and cultural groups in our country, the Government of India largely accepted this advice. I was amongst those who entirely approved. However, a visit to a remote part of our north-east frontier brought me in touch with a different point of view—the protest of the younger elements that while the rest of India was on the way to modernisation they were being preserved as museum pieces. Could we not say the same to the affluent nations?

For the last quarter of a century, we have been engaged in an enterprise unparalleled in human history—the provision of basic needs to one-sixth of mankind within the span of one or two generations. When we launched on that effort our early planners had more than the usual gaps to fill. There were not enough data and no helpful books. No guidance could be sought from the experience of other countries whose conditions—political, economic, social and technological—were altogether different. Planning, in the sense we were innovating, had never been used in the context of a mixed economy. But we could not wait. The need to improve the conditions of our people was pressing. Planning and action, improvement of data leading to better planning and better action, all this was a contin- uous and overlapping process. Our industrialisation tended to follow the paths which the more advanced countries had traversed earlier. With the advance of the sixties and particularly during the last five years, we have encountered a bewildering collection of problems, some due to our shortcomings but many inherent in the process and in existing attitudes. The feeling is growing that we should reorder our priorities and move away from the single-dimensional model which has viewed growth from certain limited angles, which seems to have given a higher place to things rather than to persons and which has increased our wants rather than our enjoyment. We should have a more comprehensive approach to life, centred on man not as a statistic but an individual with many sides to his personality. The solution of these problems cannot be isolated phenomena of marginal importance but must be an integral part of the unfolding of the very process of development.

The extreme forms in which questions of population or environmental pollution are posed obscure the total view of political, economic and social situations. The Government of India is one of the few which has an officially sponsored programme of family planning and this is making some progress. We believe that planned families will make for a healthier and more conscious population. But we know also that no programme of population control can be effective without education and without a visible rise in the standard of living. Our own programmes have succeeded in the urban or semi-urban areas. To the very poor, every child is an earner and a helper. We are experimenting with new approaches and the family planning programme is being combined with those of maternity and child welfare, nutrition and development in general.

It is an over-simplification to blame all the world's problems on increasing population. Countries with but a small fraction of the world population consume the bulk of the world's production of minerals, fossil fuels and so on. Thus we see that when it comes to the depletion of natural resources and environmental pollution, the increase of one inhabitant in an affluent country, at his level of living, is equivalent to an increase of many Asians, Africans or Latin Americans at their current material levels of living.

The inherent conflict is not between conservation and development, but between environment and the reckless exploitation of man and earth in the name of efficiency. Historians tell us that the modern age began with the will to freedom of the individual. And the individual came to believe that he had rights with no corresponding obligations. The man who got ahead was the one who commanded admiration. No questions were asked as to the methods employed or the price which others had had to pay. The industrial civilisation has promoted the concept of the efficient man, he whose entire energies are concentrated on producing more in a given unit of time and from a given unit of manpower. Groups or individuals who are less competitive and, according to this test, less efficient are regarded as lesser breeds—for example the older civilisations, the black and brown peoples, women and certain professions. Obsolescence is built into production, and efficiency is based on the creation of goods which are not really needed and which cannot be disposed of, when discarded. What price such efficiency now, and is not reckless a more appropriate term for such behaviour?

All the "isms" of the modern age—even those which in theory disown the private profit principle—assume that man's cardinal interest is acquisition. The profit motive, individual or collective, seems to overshadow all else. This overriding concern with self and today is the basic cause of the ecological crisis.

Pollution is not a technical problem. The fault lies not in science and technology as such but in the sense of values of the contemporary world which ignores the rights of others and is oblivious of the longer perspective.

There are grave misgivings that the discussion on ecology may be designed to distract attention from the problems of war and poverty. We have to prove to the deprived majority of the world that ecology and conservation will not work against their interest but will bring an improvement in their lives. To withhold technology from them would deprive them of vast resources of energy and knowledge. This is no longer feasible nor will it be acceptable.

The environmental problems of developing countries are not the side effects of excessive industrialisation but reflect the inadequacy of development. The rich countries may look upon development as the cause of environmental destruction, but to us it is one of the primary means of improving the environment for living, or providing food, water, sanitation and shelter; of making the deserts green and the mountains habitable. The research and perseverance of dedicated people have given us an insight which is likely to play an important part in the shaping of our future plans. We see that however much man hankers after material goods, they can never give him full satisfaction. Thus the higher standard of living must be achieved without alienating people from their heritage and without despoiling Nature of its beauty, freshness and purity so essential to our lives.

The most urgent and basic question is that of peace. Nothing is so pointless as modern warfare. Nothing destroys so instantly, so completely as the diabolic weapons which not only kill but maim and deform the living and the yet-to-be born; which poison the land, leaving long trails of ugliness, barrenness and hopeless desolation. What ecological project can survive a war?

It is clear that the environmental crisis which is confronting the world will profoundly alter the future destiny of our planet. No one among us, whatever our status, strength or circumstance, can remain unaffected. The process of change challenges present international policies. Will the growing awareness of "one earth" and "one environment" guide us to the concept of "one humanity"? Will there be more equitable sharing of environmental costs and greater international interest in the accelerated progress of the less developed world? Or will it remain confined to a narrow concern, based on exclusive self-sufficiency?

The first essays in narrowing economic and technological disparities have not succeeded because the policies of aid were made to subserve the equations of power. We hope that the renewed emphasis on self-reliance, brought about by the change in the climate for aid, will also promote a search for new criteria of human satisfaction. In the meantime, the ecological crisis should not add to the burdens of the weaker nations by introducing new considerations in the political and trade policies of rich nations. It would be ironic if the fight against pollution were to be converted into another business, out of which a few companies, corporations, or nations would make profits at the cost of the many. Here is a branch of experimentation and discovery in which scientists of all nations should take interest. They should ensure that their findings are available to all nations, unrestricted by patents. I am glad that the Conference has given thought on this aspect of the problem.

Life is one and the world is one, and all these questions are interlinked. The population explosion, poverty, ignorance and disease, the pollution of our surroundings, the stockpiling of nuclear weapons and biological and chemical agents of destruction are all parts of a vicious circle. Each is important and urgent but dealing with them one by one would be wasted effort.

It serves little purpose to dwell on the past or to apportion blame, for none of us is blameless. If some are able to dominate over others, this is at least partially due to the weakness, the lack of unity and the temptation of gaining some advantage on the part of those who submit. If the prosperous have been exploiting the needy, can we honestly claim that in our own societies, people do not take advantage of the weaker sections? We must re-evaluate the fundamentals on which our respective civic societies are based and the ideals by which they are sustained. If there is to be a change of heart, a change of direction and methods of functioning, it is not an organisation or a country—no matter how well intentioned—which can achieve it. While each country must deal with that aspect of the problem which is most relevant to it, it is obvious that all countries must unite in an overall endeavour. There is no alternative to a co-operative approach on a global scale to the entire spectrum of our problems.

I have referred to some problems which seem to me to be the underlying causes of the present crisis in our civilisation. This is not in the expectation that this Conference can achieve miracles or solve all the world's difficulties, but in the hope that the opinions of each nation will be kept in focus, that these problems will be viewed in perspective and each project devised as part of the whole.

On a previous occasion I have spoken of the unfinished revolution in our countries. I am now convinced that this can be taken to its culmination when it is accompanied by a revolution in social thinking. In 1968 at the 14th General Conference of UNESCO the Indian delegation, along with others, proposed a new and major programme entitled "a design for living". This is essential to grasp the full implications of technical advance and its impact on different sections and groups. We do not want to put the clock back or resign ourselves to a simplistic natural state. We want new directions in the wiser use of the knowledge and tools with which science has equipped us. And this cannot be just one upsurge but a continuous search into cause and effect and an unending effort to match technology with higher levels of thinking. We must concern ourselves not only with the kind of world we want but also with what kind of man should inhabit it. Surely we do not desire a society divided into those who condition and those who are conditioned. We want thinking people, capable of spontaneous self-directed activity, people who are interested and interesting, and who are imbued with compassion and concern for others.

It will not be easy for large societies to change their style of living. They cannot be coerced to do so, nor can governmental action suffice. People can be motivated and urged to participate in better alternatives.

It has been my experience that people who are at cross purposes with Nature are cynical about mankind and ill-at-ease with themselves. Modern man must re-establish an unbroken link with Nature and with life. He must again learn to invoke the energy of growing things and to recognise, as did the ancients in India centuries ago, that one can take from the Earth and the atmosphere only so much as one puts back into them. In their Hymn to Earth, the sages of the Atharva Veda chanted:

"What of thee I dig out, let that quickly grow over,
Let me not hit thy vitals, or thy heart."

So can man himself be vital and of good heart and conscious of his responsibility.

CHAPTER NINE

Twenty-Five Years of Independence, 1947–1972

1. ARTICLE FOR *FOREIGN AFFAIRS**

THIS YEAR INDIA CELEBRATES THE TWENTY-FIFTH ANNIVERSARY of her independence. These have been years of change and turmoil everywhere. Deep surging forces have torn asunder our past colonial feudal structures and have combined with the tides sweeping the world to give our post-independence evolution its unique qualities. But our own unvarying concerns have been two: to safeguard our independence and to overcome the blight of poverty.

Many crises and dangers from within and without have obstructed our path but we have taken them in our stride. Contrary to predictions, the country has not broken into warring states. We have not succumbed to civil anarchy. There has been no widespread starvation; on the contrary, we have become self-sufficient in cereals. We have not jettisoned our free institutions, but instead gained greater political cohesion and economic strength. This does not justify complacency but it does give us confidence that the Indian people can rise to whatever challenge the future may hold. Under Mahatma Gandhi's inspiration, Prime Minister Jawaharlal Nehru and the Congress movement formulated a set of principles which have served as our guidelines and which are still valid for us. These are democracy, socialism and secularism so far as our internal affairs are concerned, and non-alignment in our external relations. One or the other of these principles has been the subject of criticism within the country and abroad. But generally speaking, internally there is a more mature awareness of the forces and compulsions of our age, and these principles have come to form the essential elements of a national programme accepted by virtually all sections of our people, even though there are differences of

*Article for the October 1972 issue of *Foreign Affairs*.

interpretation and regarding tactics. The massive majority with which the Congress Party was returned to power in the fifth general election in 1971 and in the state elections in 1972 is an indication of this.

What holds people together is not religion, not race, not language, not even a commitment to an economic system. It is shared experience and involvement in the conscious and continuous effort at resolving internal differences through political means. It is a sense of "Indianness" which unites our people despite ethnic, linguistic and religious diversity. Most conflicts and tensions in the world originate in the failure to take note of the importance of nationalism.

Two centuries and more of history marked by foreign intervention, domination and exploitation left India backward, apathetic and stagnant. The general scene was one of decay, reflected in the misery of the masses. For us, political independence became inseparable from economic freedom, which in turn could be meaningful to the extent that it served the interests not only of the few but of the many, of the nation as a whole. Hence our energies at home have been chiefly directed toward the reconstruction of our society.

Our national movement was committed not to a doctrine but to a purpose—the modernisation of our society without loss of the Indian personality; the development and integration of industry and agriculture with modern science and technology; the uplift of the masses and the ending of archaic, hierarchical systems in which discrimination and exploitation had become entrenched.

In the economic field, it was clear from the beginning that we could not rely only on private enterprise and the play of market forces, that we would have to establish social control over the key sectors of the economy and adopt measures of economic planning appropriate to the stage of development reached. Our socialism is not a ready-made ideology but a flexible concept. Three successive Five-Year Plans have been implemented and we are halfway through the Fourth. None of them was beyond criticism in formulation or execution. And yet the overall progress of the last twenty-five years is by no means negligible. We have an impressive record of diversifying our industrial capacity and raising industrial output. The Indian peasant has quickly responded to the new strategy, with the state providing irrigation, improved seeds, better implements, fertilisers and pesticides. So marked has been the development of our industry and agriculture, our science and technology, our education and health, that some argue that India should not now be counted among the under-developed nations.

Although we have acquired certain features of an industrial state and although some classes and groups of our people are visibly prosperous, the vast majority still live in poverty and a substantial minority in crushing poverty. Moreover, the process of development has widened the disparities between different social classes and has created new imbalances between states and between districts within the same state.

Our very progress has drawn attention to the inadequacy of our achievement and to the magnitude of the tasks that still lie ahead. But it has increased our capacity to deal with them. We have realised that reliance on stereotyped processes of economic growth will not make an appreciable impact on the living conditions of the masses for decades to come. Hence, a basic review of our economic policies is now under way. We propose a more direct assault on poverty and its major manifestation, unemployment. Our next Five-Year Plan will emphasise investment and production programmes which are closely related to a minimum level of consumption for all and are linked to the provision of employment opportunities on an extensive scale. This gigantic enterprise calls for institutional changes and innovations.

These radical policies do not conform to the code of capitalism and they may not adhere to orthodox doctrines of socialism but they are desired by the great majority of our people. The privileged do not hide their misgivings. Reform, as in every country where it has been an issue, is being hotly debated. Some of the more glaring inequities of the land system, e.g. absentee landlordism, were removed immediately after Independence but the just redistribution of land and consolidation of holdings are yet to be satisfactorily completed. Industrialisation and urbanisation have given rise to new problems and have further accentuated disparities. However, our commitment to democracy is fundamental. Indian socialism is not a negation of democracy but its fulfilment, and democracy will be imperilled only in the measure by which we fail through lack of foresight or want of courage to respond to the aspirations of our people.

The resources for our economic development have come mostly from the sacrifices of our own people, but we have also received aid from abroad in the form of credits for the purchase of industrial equipment and food. Although aid was originally conceived of as external assistance for supplementing the self-help measures of developing countries, we have found that it is often used by some creditor governments as an instrument to enforce their short-term policy objectives and to secure political and economic concessions unrelated to our development. Aid is effective only if it is guided by considerations of development and when there is assurance of its continuity and not when it can be suspended or withdrawn abruptly. While aid is generally tied to purchases from donor countries, repayment under many of the agreements has to be made in freely convertible foreign currencies, adding to our burdens. At present more than half of the external assistance to us goes for repayments of earlier debts. It is our policy to reduce reliance on aid progressively. We are determined to mobilise internal resources and technological capacities more intensively.

India's foreign policy is a projection of the values which we have cherished through the centuries as well as our current concerns. We are not tied to the traditional concepts of a foreign policy designed to safeguard overseas possessions, investments, the carving out of spheres of influence and the erection of *cordons sanitaires*. We are not interested in exporting ideologies.

Our first concern has been to prevent any erosion of our independence. Therefore we could not be camp followers of any power, however rich or strong. We had equal interest in the maintenance and safeguarding of international peace as an essential condition of India's economic, social and political development. In the bipolar world which existed in the immediate postwar era, Jawaharlal Nehru refused to join either bloc. He decided to remain non-aligned as a means of safeguarding our independence and contributing to the maintenance of world peace. Non-alignment implied neither non-involvement nor neutrality. It was and is an assertion of our freedom of judgment and action. We have not hesitated to express our views on any major controversy or to support just causes.

In conformity with the objectives of our foreign policy, India sought friendship with every nation. We did not allow past conflicts to impede our new links with Britain within the framework of the Commonwealth. The problem of French possessions in India, unlike those held held by the Portuguese, was solved in a civilised manner by peaceful negotiations. Thereafter, our relations with France grew in cordiality. We have similar relations with the Federal Republic of Germany and the German Democratic Republic and other European countries, both East and West. With the non-aligned countries in Asia, the Middle East,

North Africa and Africa south of the Sahara, there exist special understanding and co-operation based on a common interest in safeguarding freedom and a common struggle against colonialism, neocolonialism and racialism. We have friendships with the countries of Latin America whose concern with problems of development is similar to ours. India has always held Japan in esteem as a dynamic Asian country, and our co-operation with Japan is steadily growing.

We have also tried to have normal relations with Pakistan. Yet successive governments of Pakistan based the survival and unity of their country on the idea of confrontation with India. This has stood in the way of co-operation which would have been to our mutual benefit. India was partitioned in 1947 to solve what the British portrayed as irreconcilable Hindu-Muslim antagonism. Pakistan was based on the medieval notion that religion alone constituted nationhood. Encouraged by the imperial power, the Muslim League claimed that Muslim majority areas were entitled to become an independent nation. Thus, Pakistan was born a geographical curiosity, its two halves separated by a thousand miles of Indian territory. India was left with a very large number of Muslims; they formed the largest of her many minorities. In keeping with her old tradition and the spirit of her nationalist movement, India adopted secularism—i.e. non-discrimination on grounds of religion—as a fundamental state principle. Equal rights and equal protection have been vouchsafed for the followers of all religions. The Muslim population of India has grown since partition from 35 million to 61 million. It is noteworthy that the 1971 census showed that there are 14 million Christians and 17 million others including Sikhs, Buddhists, Jains, Parsis and Jews.

Pakistan, on the other hand, clung to the political ideology which had led to partition. Those who came to power in Pakistan had sided with the colonial power in undivided India and had opposed the national struggle. These ruling elements, especially after the establishment of military dictatorship, set Pakistan on a course of pointless and seemingly endless conflict with India. Just as in the earlier days when the colonial power had used religious sentiments to blunt the nationalist drive in India, some powers sought to use Pakistan to offset India. Pakistan joined military alliances, which had been formed ostensibly to contain international Communism, but which Pakistan used primarily in order to acquire weapons to be used against India. Moreover, it suited the West to play off Pakistan against India. China gave military assistance to Pakistan with the same purpose. Later, so did the Soviet Union in order not to lose leverage, but soon discovered its hazards. The consequence of this assistance was to strengthen the militarist oligarchy in Pakistan and inhibit the growth of democratic forces there. Hatred and suspicion of India were whipped up to maintain those in power and to divert the Pakistani people's attention from their demands. Since India remained outside military systems, our defence capacity, unlike that of Pakistan, had to be built up out of our own resources. We have bought defence equipment from a number of countries, however, particularly after the Chinese invasion in 1962 when we received very modest assistance from the United States and the United Kingdom.

Kashmir, as early as October 1947, was the first victim of aggression by Pakistan. This was at a time when there were no Indian forces at all in Kashmir—as acknowledged by the Foreign Minister of Pakistan at that time in the UN Security Council. A large part of that state has been under Pakistan's occupation for many years. India does not intend to recapture this territory by force; on several occasions we have given this assurance to Pakistan and have offered to conclude a "no war" pact. Pakistan has rejected this offer repeatedly, trying to invoke third-party intervention in our affairs. Infiltrators and saboteurs have been sent into Kashmir and other territories, notably in the north-east. Early in 1965, our Kutch area was invaded, and later the same year the infiltration was escalated into an attack on Kashmir which led to fighting all along the western front.

The immediate background to the latest aggression against us in 1971 was the other battle which Pakistan had been waging for many months against its own citizens of East Pakistan (as it then was). India had no part in the internal developments of Pakistan—West or East. We would normally have welcomed the attainment of freedom by any victim of colonial oppression but usually it would have little direct impact on us. Bangla Desh, however, was a part of our subcontinent. How could we ignore a conflict which took place on our very border and overflowed into our own territory? Ten million destitute refugees poured into densely pop- ulated areas which were also politically sensitive owing to the activities of Marxists and the Left extremists we call Naxalites. This posed unbearable strains on our economy and on our social and administrative institutions. The terrible stories of genocide and the comings and goings of Mukti Bahini, the resistance force of Bangla Desh, created a volatile situation for us also. Could we remain indifferent to these developments?

As I told the leaders of the various countries which I visited in October 1971, the situation could not remain static. Several border clashes took place during these tense months, and there was one serious skirmish in November; but we treated these as local incidents. In the last week of November, President Yahya Khan publicly announced that war would begin in ten days and, sure enough, on the tenth day there was a massive air attack on seven of our cities and a ground attack all along our western border. Thus did Pakistan extend its war to India.

However, when fourteen days later, on December 16, 1971, Pakistani troops surrendered on the eastern front, India unilaterally announced a ceasefire on the western front also. On March 25, 1972, we withdrew our troops from Bangla Desh in consultation with the new government. The political map of the subcontinent has been redrawn and the notion of an inherent and insuperable antagonism between a secular India and a predominantly Muslim state has been discredited—not through any design on our part but because the idea itself was untenable and the military dictatorship of Pakistan, totally alienated from its own people, had followed a short-sighted and unrealistic policy. In his address to the nation on June 27, 1972, President Bhutto gave a perceptive account of the events when he said:

> The war we have lost was not of our making. I had warned against it but my warning fell on the deaf ears of a power-drunk junta. They recklessly plunged our people into the war and involved us in an intolerable surrender and lost us half our country. The junta did not know how to make peace nor did it know how to make war.

The shock of these events compelled Pakistan to exchange military dictatorship for civilian rule and opened the door to new possibilities for the peaceful resolution of the basic issues between the two countries. I took the initiative to invite President Bhutto for discussions. These have resulted in the Simla Agreement of July 2, 1972, by which Pakistan and India have proclaimed their determination to solve their conflicts bilaterally and without recourse to force, and to seek a durable peace and growing economic and cultural co-operation. The agreement, which holds the promise of settlement of the Kashmir and boundary problems, has been welcomed by almost all sections of the Indian people. It is my hope that the implementation of this agreement in the spirit in which it was made will close the twenty-five-year-old period of Pakistan's hatred of India, and that both countries will become good neighbours. I appreciate the courage and realistic approach which enabled President Bhutto to come to India. If Pakistan also shows the wisdom to come to terms with Bangla Desh which, under Sheikh Mujibur Rahman, is building a secular, socialist-oriented democracy, the subcontinent will at long last have overcome the main obstacle to its progress.

I have dwelt at length on Pakistan and the problems of the subcontinent for their impact on us is immediate and deep. But we want better relations with China also. Even when we were fully absorbed in our own struggle for liberty, we supported China's parallel fight against imperialism and sent a medical team to Mao Tse-tung's Eighth Route Army. We have respect for their culture and cherish memories of past contacts. We were among the first in 1949 to welcome the establishment of the People's Republic.

Much to our disappointment, the last two decades have failed to fulfil our initial hope that India and China, both great Asian nations newly independent and faced with similar problems, would learn from and assist each other and so co-operate on the wider international scene. We began, as we thought, with mutual confidence and goodwill, but the events of the 1950s brought tension and misunderstanding, culminating in the entry of Chinese troops and their occupation of thousands of square miles of Indian territory in 1962.

It would be an oversimplification to regard this merely as the result of a border dispute. Simultaneous or subsequent developments—such as China's systematic support of Pakistan against India, her provocative criticism of India for alleged subservience to the United States and later the Soviet Union, and her persistent though futile efforts to promote internal subversion—leave us no option but to infer that the border dispute was the outcome of a more complex policy which was aimed at undermining India's stability and at obstructing her rapid and orderly progress. After the Cultural Revolution, conditions seem more tranquil, and there appears to be a new orientation of China's policies. We wonder whether this new mood will also be reflected in China's policy toward India. The earlier faint signs of a thaw have receded since China's unreserved support of General Yahya Khan's campaign against Bangla Desh and India. We are not engaged in any competition with China, nor have we any hostile intentions. We hope that some day China will appreciate that co-operative and freindly relations between the 560 million people of India and the 700 million people of China are in our mutual interest.

Apart from the Soviet leaders, I think my father was the first Prime Minister to pay a state visit to China. Similarly, the exchange of visits with the leaders of the Soviet Union was memorable in that it was the first time since the October Revolution that a non-Communist personality of Nehru's stature and the head of a non-Communist government was welcomed officially by the Soviet government; it was the first time, also, that Soviet leaders travelled in a country outside the Socialist bloc. The talks held in Moscow and Delhi resulted in a significant measure of understanding that had more than bilateral implications. They demonstrated that it was possible for two countries such as India and the Soviet Union to maintain good relations and to work together in a friendly spirit in spite of very different social systems and without either having to modify its policies or sacrifice its philosophy and traditions.

The Soviet Union shares the Indian view on the maintenance of peace and the elimination of racialism and colonialism. On these issues it has supported the Afro-Asian stand in the United Nations and elsewhere. When matters vitally concerning our national security and integrity, such as Goa, Kashmir and more lately Bangla Desh, became subjects of international controversy, the Soviet assessment of the merits of the case coincided largely with our own. In strictly bilateral terms also, there has been a steady increase in the range and volume of our co-operation— economic, commercial and cultural—to our mutual advantage. Economic relations with the Soviet Union are easier for us since we repay them through the export of our commodities. This mode of payment makes the Soviet credits self-liquidating.

The Treaty of Peace, Friendship and Co-operation concluded last year grew logically from this expanding relationship. It affirms the determination of both countries for greater co-operation in various fields and to consult one another, if need be, on suitable measures to safeguard their peace and security. There is nothing in the treaty to which any reasonable person or government could take exception. It contains no secret clauses, nor is it aimed against any country. Yet there have been some misapprehensions that the treaty dilutes India's non-alignment. It is strange that such criticism comes mostly from those who have vehemently denounced non-alignment all along. In the text of the treaty itself there is explicit recognition and endorsement of India's policy of non-alignment.

Our relations with the United States started off rather well. At that time, the American people and government showed considerable sympathy for the colonial peoples who were struggling for independence, and particularly for India. However, this phase was short-lived. With the rise of the United States to a dominant world position, Washington's concern and respect for the national independence of India receded into the background. Everything was viewed solely in the context of checking Communism and containing first the Soviet Union, subsequently China, and now once again the Soviet Union. There was a feverish building of military blocs and a continuous extension of a network of bases stretching across oceans and continents. The logical and practical consequence of this policy was to divide the world into two opposing camps and to expect each country to belong to one or the other—preferably the Western bloc.

A newly freed people, jealous of their independence, could not resign themselves to this position, nor could we isolate ourselves from what was happening around us. Successive U.S. administrations have ignored the fact that India must see her problems and her relationships in a different perspective. They have insisted on interpreting our non-alignment within the confines of a neutralism which they imagined to be slanted in favour of Russia. India was regarded with disapproval and resentment because of her independent policy. This could not but affect the bilateral relations between India and America. Despite fluctuations of mood, our relationship as a whole has been uneasy over a long period.

To our grave concern, U.S. policy as it developed impinged seriously on our vital interests. The admission of Pakistan into the U.S. controlled system of alliances and the massive supply of arms to Pakistan were ostensibly part of the U.S. grand design against Communism, but we cannot believe that the U.S. administration was unaware that these weapons could be and would be used only against India. We took considerable pains to point this out but our protests went unheeded.

Should not the people of the United States ask their government what they have gained from America's activities in Europe and in Asia? Has the United States succeeded in containing Communism? On the contrary, has not the U.S. government been compelled to build bridges with the non-aligned and to woo the opposite bloc—the hated Communists? I have no doubt that if we had followed the advice of the Western bloc conditions in India would have deteriorated and the extremists would have been strengthened.

In regard to Bangla Desh and during the December war, the United States openly backed Pakistan at the cost of basic human values. This further strained our relations. I do not wish to analyse the U.S. role at that time or go into the misrepresentations which were circulated. But it is necessary to take note of the dispatch of the warship *Enterprise* to support a ruthless military dictatorship and to intimidate a democracy, and the extraordinary similarity of the attitudes adopted by the United States and China. Imagine our feelings. The original misunderstanding with the United States had arisen because of our contacts with China, the Soviet Union and Eastern Europe. We find it difficult to understand why, when the U.S. policy toward these countries changed, the resentment against us increased.

We do not believe in permanent estrangement. We admire the achievements of the American people. Indeed, a large number of Americans expressed sympathetic support for the cause of Bangla Desh and India during the last year. We are grateful for the assistance from the United States in many areas of our development. We are ready to join in any serious effort to arrive at a deeper appreciation of each other's point of view and to improve relations. A great power must take into account the existence not only of countries with comparable power, but of the multitude of others who are no longer willing to be pawns on a global chessboard. Above all, the United States has yet to resolve the inner contradiction between the traditions of the founding fathers and of Lincoln and the external image it gives of a superpower pursuing the cold logic of power politics.

On fundamental questions such as disarmament, the abolition of nuclear weapons, the continuing struggle against colonialism and racialism, the widening gulf between the haves and have nots, the war in Vietnam and the conflict in the Middle East, our stand has been consistent over the years and has been clearly stated in appropriate forums. In this article I have preferred to focus attention on the situation on our subcontinent because it is our special concern and has a significance beyond geographical frontiers. In considering the policies of some major powers, I have confined myself to bilateral relations which are intimately connected with their attitudes to the subcontinent as a whole.

The international scene with which we had become familiar has considerably altered. Do the two recent summit meetings in Peking and Moscow indicate that Communism and anti-Communism will no longer be the ultimate criteria of political and moral values and that peaceful coexistence, which India has been advocating all these years, will be the governing consideration in international dealings? Whatever the motivation, the wisdom of these new approaches is beyond question, provided that the spirit of detente is also extended to other parts of the world. We cannot be sure if these flexible relationships necessarily point to a more stable world order. Coexistence by itself does not preclude policies, separately or in concert, which are detrimental to the freedom and interests of third countries. For example, co-ordinated action in the Security Council between China and the United States last year operated against an immediate restoration of peace in Bangla Desh in keeping with the rights of its people. Agreements which promote the doctrine of balance of power or mark out spheres of influence are bound to increase tension and invite instability. No nation will be happy in a subservient role.

Europe has avoided war for more than two decades and is now attempting to build a framework of security and co-operation. But peace is indivisible and so long as there are conflicts and dissensions in Asia there will be no peace in the world. Asia has cradled many civilisations and contains a substantial section of the world's population. For more than two centuries, it has been drained of its resources and wealth which have contributed in no small measure to the industrial advance and affluence of the West. The countries of Asia are now politically free but the continuing interplay of international forces impedes our struggle against economic backwardness and the shadows of the past. We share many problems which can be solved through co-operation among ourselves rather than merely through assistance from the outside, which has tended to cause misunderstanding among us and which was motivated more by self-interest than by a genuine understanding of our needs.

Each country has its own heritage and distinct personality which it naturally wishes to develop in its own way. But we must also bear in mind our community of interests and take positive initiatives for working together among ourselves and with other countries in order to make a richer contribution toward the evolution of a world more livable for all and of a social order more in consonance with the yearnings of modern man.

2. SPEECH AT MIDNIGHT SESSION OF PARLIAMENT, AUGUST 14–15, 1972

We have gathered from all parts of the country to live again a moment of history when, out of the long gloom of feudalism and foreign rule, India awoke to freedom and democracy. We have come to remember with gratitude the long succession of those who have gone before us. The Father of the Nation reinterpreted our ancient values and traditions and transformed ideals that seemed unattainable into powerful instruments of political action. His message reached out to village and town, inspired the educated, brought understanding to the simplest and awakened long suppressed aspirations.

Our movement was a non-violent one. It released unthought of qualities in our people and revealed the many faces of courage. By participating in a cause larger than himself, every Indian grew in stature. Some groups followed the more familiar path of armed confrontation. Many were the instances of individual daring and self-sacrifice. I recall also the work of the Indian National Army away from our shores.

My mind goes still further back, beyond personal memory, to the great rising of 1857. The immediate cause does not matter. Perhaps deep in the subconscious, underlying sentiments of caste and religion was another stirring, the search for identity.

It was a remarkable century. The darkness of oppression was illumined by great intellects. Men of religion were also revolutionaries. Poets, scientists, indeed people of all professions, were one in a great objective—the resurgence of the nation.

Ultimately, success was achieved by the countless men and women, unknown and unsung who served our cause by their numbers no less than their dedication.

What was our strength? Oppressed and humiliated as we were, our leaders raised us above fear and hate. Transcending all hardship, we focussed our gaze on a vision of the future. We had faith that a people who moved with dignity and courage could not be cowed; that India awakened could never again be subdued.

We have always believed that freedom is indivisible. We have been in touch with movements for liberation everywhere and have contributed to them. Today we reaffirm our solidarity with the many Asian and African countries which became free with us or soon after, the latest of whom is Bangla Desh, and with all those who are still struggling for freedom or development.

At the moment of Independence, our energies turned from the tension of struggle to the immediate problems of partition and the vast new responsibilities which we had assumed. That night, Jawaharlal Nehru said in a mood of prophecy: "The future is not one of ease or resting but of incessant striving so that we may fulfil the pledges that we have so often taken." A quarter of a century has since elapsed, during which we have had our share of failure and success, of tragedy and triumph. And yet we can take pride in the undeniable fact that despite the long sequence of challenges, we are today stronger—politically, economically, and socially. *Our national unity, democracy, secularism and socialism remain strong and firm.*

Our quest has been friendship with all, submission to none. Our fight was not for ourselves alone but for all mankind. Nor was it merely for political independence in its narrow sense. We were determined to change the old order, to eradicate poverty, to emancipate society from rigid stratification, evil customs and superstition.

The struggle for freedom began when the first man was enslaved and it will continue until the last man is freed not merely of visible bondage but of the concepts of inferiority due to race, colour, caste or sex. Only those who are free in spirit can be the torch bearers of freedom and pioneers of the future.

The greatness for which we strive is not the arrogance of military power or the avarice of economic exploitation. It is the true greatness of the spirit which India has cherished through the millennia. Man in the nuclear age stands at a crucial crossroads in his destiny. Let us rededicate ourselves not only to the service of India and her great people, but beyond to the broader goals of world peace and human welfare so that generations yet unborn can live with dignity and fulfilment, as part of the great world family.

Index

Abraham, K. C., 113
Administration, 69–70, 113, 115
Africa, 30, 126, 130, 133–34, 139, 141–42, 149, 156, 181, 195, 207, 211, 261
Agra, 170, 173
Agriculture, 52, 70, 76–78, 80–81; land reform, 106, 108; research, 162, 204
Ali, Sadiq, 105
Alice in Wonderland (Carroll), 55
Allahabad, 16–19, 43
All-India Conference on Family Planning, 77
All-India Congress Committee (A.I.C.C.), 97–111, 113, 116
All-India Institute of Medical Science, 72, 76
Ambala, 170, 173
Amrakunja Samavartana, Santiniketan, 62
Amritsar, 170, 173
Anand Bhawan, 16
Angola, 126, 141
Animals, 39–40, 191
Apartheid, 142, 144
Artificial Limb Centre, Poona, 41
Asia, 30, 130, 132–34, 139, 142, 144, 155–56, 162, 164, 181, 195, 206–07, 210–12, 214, 216
Ashoka, 28, 89, 140, 192
Assam, 39
Atharva-Veda, 199
Atomic Energy Establishment, 53, 67
Aurora, Lt.-Gen. Jagjit Singh, 174
Austria, 155, 159–60, 163, 173

Austrian Society for Foreign Policy and International Relations, 154n
Austrian State Treaty, 160
Avantipur, 170, 173
Awami League, 160, 163, 169

Banaras (Varanasi, Kashi, Benares), 88–92
Bangalore, 97, 173
Bangla Desh (East Bengal, East Pakistan), 160–62, 164–65, 169–75, 185, 208–11, 213–14, 216
Banks, nationalisation of, 84, 86, 97, 107–09
Bengal, 15, 62–63, 79, 173
Belgium, 163, 173
Bentham, Jeremy, 182
Besant, Annie, 89
Bhabha, Dr. Homi, 53
Bhutto, President, 209–10
Bihar, 86–87
Bombay, 15–16, 79, 87, 112, 173
Britain, *see* United Kingdom
Buddha, Gautama, 91, 140, 150
Buddhists, 38, 89, 155, 161, 207

Calcutta, 15, 79, 173
Cambodia, 144
Canada, 19
Caribbean Islands, 142
Caste, 82–83, 99, 158, 182, 185–86
Census (1971), 162
Children, 39, 42–43, 74
China, 207–8, 210–14

Christians, 155, 161, 207
Churchill, Winston, 58
Colonialism, 122, 126, 128, 130–32,
    141, 144–45, 150–51, 181–82, 189, 207,
    211–13
Commonwealth, 206
Communism, 99, 103, 207, 211–13
Conference of Non-aligned Nations
    (1969), 139–40
Conference on Human Environment
    (U.N.), 191–92
Conference on Science and Technology,
    68–69
Congo, 149
Congress, Indian National, 13n, 44–46,
    81, 85–88, 97–116, 131–41, 156, 183,
    189, 203–04
Constitution, Indian, 82–83, 115, 155,
    157–58, 161–62, 184
Corinthians, 63
Czechoslovakia, 127

Dacca, 161, 170, 174
Dalai Lama, 38
Darwin, Charles, 188
Das, Dr. Bhagwan, 89, 92
Delhi (& New Delhi), 23–24, 42, 79,
    87, 97, 119n, 174, 211
Democracy, 61, 63–64, 81–82, 101, 111,
    115, 156, 159, 161–62, 164, 181–84,
    190, 203, 205, 216
Desai, Morarji, 97
Deva, Narendra, 92
Development Decades (U.N.), 119–24,
    146, 151
Dharma, 90
Dickens, Charles, 56
Disarmament, 127, 143, 213
Dravida Munnetra Kazzagham (D.M.K.),
    88

East Bengal Pakistan, see Bangla Desh
Eastern Bloc, 132–33
Economic development, 53, 67, 79,
    101–02, 108, 150–51, 159, 182, 184,
    195, 204
Education, 55–62, 64–65, 71, 74, 78, 129,
    159, 182–83, 187, 195
Electronics, 67
Eliot, T. S., 64–65

Engineering, 68, 70–71
Enterprise (U.S. warship), 213
Environment, 71, 147, 191–99
Europe, East, 74, 213
Europe, West, 67–68, 132, 155–56, 160,
    163, 184, 187, 212
Everest, Mount, 192
Experts, 69

Family Planning, 47, 75–80, 162, 195
Finance Commission, 158
Five Year Plans, 53, 67–68, 304–05
Foodgrains, 52, 159, 162, 203
Foreign policy (non-alignment), 86, 99,
    105, 109, 111, 119–20, 131–44, 159,
    211–12
France, 13, 81, 83, 144, 173, 190, 206
Freedom, 60, 64, 183–84, 186

Galileo, 142
Gandhi, Feroz, 16–18
Gandhi, Indira: youth, 14–15; arrest and
    imprisonment, 16–19; hostess, 37–39,
    42; policy, 51–54; Acharya, Visva-
    Bharati, 61; philosophy, 63–64, 71,
    90–92, 98; Congress Committee, 97–98;
    freedom fight, 186
Gandhi, Mohandas Karamchand (Bapu,
    Gandhiji, Mahatma), 13, 22, 24–30,
    46, 51, 63–64, 66, 81–82, 85, 89–92,
    99–100, 104, 110–11, 125, 130–31,
    140, 158, 182, 184, 186, 192, 203, 215
Gandhi, Rajiv, 25, 39, 42–43
Gandhi, Sanjay, 39, 42–43
Ganga (Ganges), 66, 89–90, 92
Gaza Strip, 149
General elections, 155, 162, 186, 204
Geneva Convention, 174
Germany, 135, 173, 206
Giri, V. V., 97
Gita, 175
Goa, 211
Gokhale, Gopal Krishna, 28
Gopal, Dr., 34
Gorakhpur District, 56, 73n
Gruber, (Austrian Foreign Minister), 160
Guinea Bissau, 142
Gurudev, 15, 62–63, 65
Guyana, 146

Harijans, 82–83

Himalayas, 65

Hindus, 37, 90, 92, 155, 161, 207

Husain, Dr. Zaikir, 97

Imports, 159, 206

Independence, 23, 44–45, 47, 81, 83, 102, 183, 216

India International Centre, 80n

Indian armed forces, 174–76

Indian Council for Cultural Relations, 80n

Indian Mutiny, 215

Indian National Army, 215

Indian Ocean, 144–45

Indian Political Science Conference, 185–91

Indo-China, 144, 149

Indo-French Colloquium, 80, 88

Indus, 66

Industrial Revolutions, 56, 67, 184, 188

Industry, 52, 82, 107–08, 159, 194–96, 204; industrial design, 70

Intelligentsia, 74, 84, 114, 161, 187–88

The International, 37n

International aid, 124–31, 203, 205–06

International affairs, 53, 172

International Club, Bombay, 37n

International Commission of Non-aligned countries, 144

International Planned Parenthood Federation, 77

Israel, 144

Jails, *see* Prisons

Jain (A.P.) Committee, 75

Jains, 155, 207

Jallianwala Bagh, 26

Jana Sangh Party, 85–86, 103, 106–07

Japan, 67, 79, 190, 207

Jarring, Ambassador, 126

Jawaharlal Nehru Memorial Trust, 31, 33–34

Jews, 207

Jodhpur, 170, 173

Kabir, 76, 89, 91

Kanchipuram, 91

Kashi Vidyapith, 88–90, 92

Kashmir, 173, 208–09, 211

Kerala, 52, 88

Khadi, 13–14, 24; "Gandhi cap", 32

Khemkaran, 170

Khosla, Dr. A. N., 66

Khrushchev, Nikita, 160

Kissinger, Dr., 173

Korea, 149

Kutch, 208

Lakshmi Bai, Rani of Jansi, 46

Land system, 157, 182, 205

Language, 57, 61, 82, 135, 188

Laos, 144

Latin America, 142, 195, 207

Law, rule of, 182–83, 188

League of Nations, 147–48

Lincoln, Abraham, 213

Literacy, 156, 187

Lok Sabha, 97, 215

Lucknow, 24

Lusaka Conference of Non-aligned Countries, 139–41, 149–50

Macaulay, Lord, 182

Madras, 55–57, 68

Magadha, 91

Malaviya, Madan Mohan, 89

Manipur, 91

Mao Tse-tung, 210

Marcuse, Herbert, 91

Marx, Karl, 30, 182; Marxists, 208

Masani, Minoo, 85

Mass media, 80, 142, 172

Mavalankar Hall, 131

Medicine, 72–73; disease, 73, 75–76, 197; doctors, 72–74, 79; hospitals, 95; medical education, 74; specialisation, 74

Middle East, *see* West Asia

Mill, John Stuart, 182

Missouri, University of, 80

Moscow, 211, 213

Moshai, Master, 62

Mozambique, 126, 141

Mukti Bahini, 170, 174, 176, 208

Muslims, 23–24, 38, 88, 155, 161, 207, 209

Muslim League, 207

Mysore, 97

Naidu, Sarojini, 13

Naini Tal, 39, 59

Namibia, 142

Nanak, 91
Nasser, President, 144
National Development Council, 53, 158
National Integration Council, 158
Nationalism, 204
National Planning Committee, 67
National Press Club, Washington, 162
Naxalites, 208
Nehru, Shrimati (w.o. Jawaharlal), 13–15
Nehru, Shrimati (w.o. Motilal), 15
Nehru, B. K., 46
Nehru, Jawaharlal, 15, 24–26, 29–34,
    42, 44, 51, 54, 63–64, 71, 81–82, 85, 92,
    97, 102, 111–12, 120, 124–25, 133, 140,
    143, 149, 156, 160, 173, 182, 192, 203,
    206, 211, 216
Nehru, Motilal, 13, 26, 59, 60
Niazi, Lt.-Gen. A. A. K., 174
Nijalingappa, S., 97–98, 113–14
Nixon, President, 148, 171–74
Non-alignment, see Foreign Policy
North Africa, 207
North-East Frontier Area (N.E.F.A.), 87
Nuclear power, 127, 142, 147, 150, 197,
    213
Nuclear Test Ban Treaty, 150
Nutritional Research Laboratory, 75–76

Organisation Congress, 98, 104
Outer space, 154

Pakistan, West, 23, 160–61, 163–64,
    169–70, 172–77, 185, 207–10, 212–13
Palestine, 144
Panchayat system, 182
Pande, G., 66
Parsis, 155, 207
Parliamentary system, 157
Pathankot, 170, 173
Patil, Veerendra, 113
Patna, 173
Peace, 141–47, 206, 211
Peace, Friendship and Co-operation,
    Treaty of, 211
Peking, 213
Pethick-Lawrence, F. W., 17
Pharmaceutical industry, 31, 74
Planning Commission, 60, 67
Police, 18
Politics, 84–88, 155–57, 162, 185–91

Pondicherry, 88
Poona, 41
Poonch, 170
Population, 47, 76, 152, 195, 197
Portugal, 206
Portuguese Guinea, 126
Poverty, 72–74, 79–80, 82–84, 99, 119–24,
    161, 176, 193, 196–97, 205
Press, 85, 108, 160, 162–63, 172, 184, 187
Princes (Indian), 157
Prisons, 15, 17–19, 30
Problem-setters, 68–69
Prohibition, 24
Public Health, 159
Punjab, 23, 91

Quit India Movement, 16–18

Race, 82, 126, 142–44, 150, 204, 207, 211,
    213
Radhakrishnan, Dr. S., 25n, 90
Rahman, Sheikh Mujibur, 160–61, 164–65,
    169, 172, 175, 210
Ramakrishna Math, Calcutta, 15
Rama Rau, Shrimati Dhanvanthi, 77
Reddy, N. Sanjiva, 97
Refugees, 159, 161, 163–64, 169, 172, 175,
    208
Religion, 24, 28, 39, 85–86, 155, 182,
    185, 204
Research, 68, 74, 76, 80, 159, 162, 187,
    204
Riots, 40, 100
Roorkee University, 65–66, 71
Roosevelt, Franklin D., 147
Roshni, 15
Rousseau, Jean-Jacques, 182
Roy, Raja Rammohun, 89
Royal Institute of International Affairs
    (London), 181–85
Ruling Congress, 98
Rural Self-governing Councils, 155

Santiniketan, 15, 62–65
Sarnath, 89
Satya, 41
Satyagraha, 64
Science, 68, 71–72
Secularism, 82, 100–01, 111, 203, 207,
    209–10, 216

Shankaracharya, 89
Sharma, 140
Shastri, Lal Bahadur, 16, 51, 54, 89
Sikhs, 155, 207
Simla Agreement, 209
Singh, Baldev, 41
Singh, Dr. Karan, 33
Singh, Swaran, 140, 176
Snow, Lord, 80
Socialism, 36, 82, 85, 98–102, 108, 111,
114, 159, 161, 184, 203, 205, 210, 216
South Africa, 28, 89, 126, 142, 144, 150
South America, 130
South-East Asia, 144
South-West Africa, 126
Soviet Union, 30, 67–68, 74, 133–35,
139, 160, 208, 210–13
Srinagar, 170, 173
Stalingrad, 135
States, Indian, 157, 204
Subramaniam, Shri, 105
Sulaimanki, 170
Superstition, 71–73
Swaraj Bhavan, 16
Swatantra Party, 85, 87
Sweden, 39
Switzerland, 160, 176

Tagore, Rabindranath, 26, 41, 102, 124,
182
Technology, 53, 66–68, 70–72, 194
Third World, 142
Thompson, Edward, 192
Tito, Marshal, 40, 160
Transport, 52
Tribal groups, 39, 193–94

Unemployment, 106
Unfinished Revolution, 145, 147, 150, 153
United Kingdom, 19, 26, 28, 30, 56,

67–68, 71, 73, 91, 144, 156–57, 173,
182–83, 185, 190, 206–08
United Nations, 48, 119–31, 144–54, 164,
176, 191–92, 208, 211, 214
United Provinces, see Uttar Pradesh
United States of America, 44n, 52, 68,
71, 80–81, 133, 139, 144, 148, 162,
171–74, 190, 208, 210, 212–14
Universities, see Intelligentsia
U Nu, 40
Upanishads, 91; Maitri, 154
U.S.S.R., see Soviet Union
Uttar Pradesh, 39, 56, 59
Uttarlai, 170, 173

Varanasi, see Banares
Vedas, 91, 199
Vietnam, 126, 142, 144, 148
Viswa Bharati, 15, 62, 65
Vivekananda, 91
Voltaire, 182

War, 170–73, 176, 208–10, 213
Weber, Max, 182
West Asia (Middle East), 101, 126, 135,
148, 206, 213
Western Bloc, 132–33
Wilde, Oscar, 17
Women in India, 37, 46–47, 153, 158
Women on the March, 16n
Women's National Press Club,
Washington, 44n
Wordsworth, William, 41
World Wars: I, 67; II, 147

Yahya Khan, General, 170, 172, 209–10

Zimbabwe, 142
Zohra (wardress, Allahabad), 18
Zoroastrians, see Parsis.